# VEGETABLES,
# CHICKENS
# &
# BEES

# VEGETABLES, CHICKENS & BEES

AN HONEST GUIDE TO GROWING
YOUR OWN FOOD ANYWHERE

## Carson Arthur

appetite

by RANDOM HOUSE

Appetite by Random House® and colophon are registered trademarks of Penguin Random House LLC.

Library and Archives Canada Cataloguing in Publication is available upon request.

ISBN: 978-0-14-753061-5
eBook ISBN: 978-0-14-753062-2

Book and cover design by Lisa Jager
Photography by Carson Arthur, except for the following pages: Michelle Arbus: vi, 62, 63, 78, 79, 112, 162, 233, 234; Kevin Lockwood: viii, 21, 32, 73, 144, 193, 219, 231; Pixabay (ShireShy: 4; marinamarusya13: 6; alex80: 17; Freja: 38; Goumbik: 85; TANITAMON: 109; PublicDomainPictures: 126; rihaij: 129; juliacasado1: 133); Huntstock / Getty: 8; Unsplash (Clint McKoy: 10; Chad Stembridge: 11; Zanda Photography: 18; Annie Spratt: 36, 37; Markus Spiske: 48, 69; Francesco Gallarotti: 50; Johnson Chou: 83; Natalia Fogarty: 94; Harshal S Hirve: 114; Nathan Hulsey: 120; Vesela Vaclavikova: 120; Matt Montgomery: 130; Lars Blankers: 136; Rachael Gorjestani: 139, 211; Samuel Foster: 147; Dan Gold: 158; Anda Ambrosini: 161; Monika Grabkowska: 242; Marina Khrapova: 232); Johnny C.Y. Lam: 27, 89, 190, 202; Flickr (Thomas Kriese: 34; Sean Freese: 40); Sveten / Shutterstock: 53; Lindsay Vermeulen: 56; Joanna Malinowska / Freestocks: 108; R Lockwood: 230

Printed and bound in Canada

Published in Canada by Appetite by Random House®, a division of Penguin Random House Canada Limited.

www.penguinrandomhouse.ca

10  9  8  7  6  5  4  3  2  1

appetite
by RANDOM HOUSE | Penguin
Random House
Canada

How do you dedicate a book to just one person

when so many make it happen?

This one is for all of those who've had my

back, pushed me to do more and

led the way through your own hard work.

Most of all, it's for my partner, Kevin:

thank you for trusting me that a farm

was a WAY better option than

a house in the city.

TABLE
OF
CONTENTS

# INTRODUCTION

I love growing my own food. I know that the flavors are better and the food is healthier than anything I could buy in a store. Taking a tiny seed and nurturing it is incredibly rewarding—the taste of the first tomato that you grow validates all the hard work that goes into producing it!

And these rewards aren't limited to owners of sprawling yards—you can grow your own food in pretty much any space. Whether you have a small window box, a community garden plot, a big backyard, a farm of multiple acres or a patio with just a few pots, there are always options open to you, and the security that comes from knowing you're equipped to feed yourself and your family—with nothing more than some sunshine, water, dirt and seeds—goes a long way!

6 years ago, I bought a small plot of land 2 hours outside the city. I wanted to try my hand at having my own farm. I even managed to convince my partner, who is as "city" as they come, to do it with me. To be fair, I do have a little background knowledge to go on. Not only am I a landscape designer by trade but I also grew up on an apple farm. I learned how to grow stuff from an early age with the help of my mom and my grandma. We ate what we grew and put away for the winter so that we'd have our own supply all year long. When I grew up and moved away from the apple trees and into the city, growing things stayed with me.

With farming in my blood, I have traveled back and forth across the country for the past 17 years, helping people create the outdoor spaces of their dreams. I have been showing people how to make the most of whatever space they have, and how to find balance between their own human needs and those of the world around us all. I've seen how gardens can grow in all kinds of places and climates. I've also witnessed an awful lot about what *not* to do if you want your garden to survive—and thrive. Like the fact that you should call to check the locations of cable wires and gas lines *before* you start digging; like understanding the growing process is more than just sticking plants in the dirt; like avoiding angry queen bees; like the fact that absolutely everything wants to kill your chickens.

I've learned a lot working on my own garden, and in this book I am passing my advice and experience on to you so you can avoid a whole bunch of the *#gardenfail*s I've already made. First, I'll show you to look at your space and truly understand it. I'll help you assess the sunlight and the dirt; show you how to get seeds started; help you protect your garden from pests; teach you when to water your garden; and give you DIY guides for raised planters, composters and self-watering systems, to name just a few. Then I'll give my advice for growing 20 key veggies (from preparing the dirt, to harvesting them, to prepping your seeds for next year). Parts 2 and 3 are a primer on chickens and bees: Advice on choosing the right breeds for you, how to feed, care and collect from both, and some hard truths about why you might not be ready for this step yet. Plus my fav recipes for cooking all those gorgeous veggies, and what to do with the eggs and honey you collect from your chickens and bees.

Many of us (me included) have been feeling a pull toward becoming more self-sufficient in sourcing our own food and are looking at how we can use our own spaces to grow that food. Some people have called it the "grow it yourself" movement; others think it's some sort of fallout from all the "end of days" movies and TV shows. Whatever the reason, if you're keen to jump on board, my advice can help you ease into this way of life as smoothly as possible. I warn you though—this is *not* a dreamy look at an adorable Instagram-ready farm. I don't gloss over the dirty bits, but literally go into the shit you need to know (see page 80 for a guide to choosing manure!) and share my honest experience of growing food in every space.

Happy growing! And keep me posted on how it goes . . .

@carsonarthur
Carson Arthur
carsonarthur123

VEGETABLES:
YOUR
GARDEN

Thinking of starting a vegetable garden?

Whether you're a newbie or a pro, there's

always something to learn from someone else's

approach to growing vegetables.

This section covers all the basics you'll

need for any size of garden, be it a balcony,

a backyard or a community garden plot.

Good luck!

# FIRST THINGS FIRST

So you want to grow your own food? There are a few things you should know before you start digging, because things like soil, light and location all matter—a lot. Knowing what will likely work in your space *before* you start helps tip the odds toward success, rather than just set you up for a *#gardenfail*. (I've had a few of those myself, so no judgment here.)

Ultimately, whatever space you have can work so long as you understand the fundamentals of what it takes for food to grow. Don't assume you need to have a giant backyard to be successful, or even a patch of soil for that matter. Planting food on a balcony or a rooftop definitely has its challenges, but these shouldn't stop you from giving it a go! We live in all kinds of spaces, from tiny studios to huge homesteads, and any spot *with some sun* can be an opportunity to grow your own food.

## Sunlight

The most important thing to understand is sunlight. Every single plant needs some form of light to grow (and before you say "Mushrooms!" let me tell you that even they need *some* light). Put simply: If a plant doesn't have light, it won't grow. A plant's leaves are like little solar panels, converting sunshine into energy to make the plant grow. Some plants make more energy than others (and so grow faster) simply because their leaves are better at processing light.

So how much light do you need? Well, the very best growing conditions you can ask for are full sun, all day, because that gives you maximum light. Sadly, we can't always get what we want. (Yes, there's a song in there somewhere!) Instead, you work with what you've got and make smart decisions when planning what to plant and where. For sure it's tougher to grow food in a spot that only gets indirect light or is always in the shade. But there are also lots of awesome plants that grow well in shadier spots, like near a tree or even on a north-facing balcony. Certain groups of vegetables can handle more shade than others and still produce a good crop. The key to success is understanding how much sun you have in your space.

## Measuring Sunlight

There is nothing complicated about measuring sunlight—all you need is a solar-powered toy (one that operates by light and doesn't have a battery), easily found at a dollar store. So long as the toy has a little solar panel on the front or top, it will work for testing the sunlight levels in your space.

Put the toy in the spot where you are thinking of planting. Pick the spot where you think your garden will have most success. Take into consideration the various types of sun and shade you think the space may get throughout the day and the surrounding foliage also. For example, it is easier to grow vegetables under tall trees that cast dappled shade than it is under smaller trees with dense branches close to the ground. Make sure to pick an average weather day to get a true reading, because lots of clouds mean less light.

Set a reminder on your phone to check the toy once an hour, every hour, for an entire day (during the time the sun is up) and record when the toy is moving. This will give you a good understanding of how many hours of sunlight the spot will get in a day. If there is enough sunlight to make the toy move, there is enough sunlight to grow plants.

# WHAT CAN I PLANT?

Once you know how many hours of sun you average per day, you can start to think about what to grow. Here is my rule of thumb for what works best, based on the hours of sunlight in your space:

## >6 hours sunlight

Plant anything you want! The world is your oyster so take advantage of it! But don't gloat; Mother Nature has a habit of coming back and kicking you in the ass when you get too cocky.

## 4 to 6 hours sunlight

You are going to have to scale back a little. Any plants that require heat to make them sweet—like tomatoes and peppers—aren't going to love your quasi-shade garden. The general rule is that if you eat what comes *off* the plant (instead of the actual plant), you need full sun. So beans, corn and peas, for example, all need full sun for best success. They may still produce some fruit in a low-light situation, it just won't be as much. Instead, consider below-ground vegetables like onions and shallots. They handle lower-light conditions very well.

## 2 to 4 hours sunlight

Dark leafy things only. Big leaves are better at creating energy from less sun (kind of like a big solar panel versus a little one). So plants like cucumbers, zucchinis, lettuces and chards all do well in low-light situations. Even plants like carrots and beets can handle less light because they produce *a lot* of vegetation above ground. The full list of veggies that play well with little light: celery, chard, cucumbers, kale, lettuce, onions, radicchio, scallions, spinach and zucchini.

## <2 hours sunlight

This probably isn't the book for you. *Just kidding!* If your spot really doesn't get much sunlight, stick to the plants that have dark-green leaves and set your expectations low. Also get to know the farmers at your local market or investigate local community gardens.

# Dirt

Dirt (or *soil*, for those who are fanatical about their gardening terms) will always be one of the most important factors in your growing success. Soil—a mix of nutrients, minerals, organisms, gases and liquids—is the basis for supporting all life on our planet. There isn't one perfect mix of soil for growing all food, but some blends are definitely better than others.

If you are planning to grow food in a pot or planter—i.e., you will be buying your dirt rather than using the existing ground—skip ahead to page 16, where I talk about buying dirt. But if you're getting a shovel and digging out your garden, it's time to talk. Before you start any of the hard work, let's check out the ground first.

## The Dirt on Dirt

Knowing the quality of your soil really matters, not just because of the impact it has on your growing success but also because anything that is in it will end up IN your food. Learn as much as you can about the history of your space; talk to your neighbors and do your research.

If you find out that the soil used to be farmland or something agricultural, then you are golden, as odds are the soil is pretty good for growing things. But if its past life was as soil below a gas station or factory or anything else that might have contaminated it, you'll probably want to rethink planting straight in the ground. Chemicals and heavy metals can remain in the soil for many years, and you run the risk of them being absorbed by your plants and ending up in your dinner.

Getting to know the dirt in your garden will also reduce a lot of hardship when it comes time for planting, so have a good look at what is going on in the space right now. (Does the grass look super happy? Are there lots of weeds? Are there dead brown patches all over the place?) The perfect spot for a garden is where plant life is already thriving. Planting in an existing happy space will mean a lot less work for you in the long run, as nature is clearly already providing the plants what they need to survive. Ground that is dry and looks kind of dead will make your life significantly harder. Not impossible, but harder.

## Testing Your Dirt

Then comes the dirt test. You need to wait for 3 full days of sunlight in a row with no rain to do this one. Once the ground is nice and dry, take out one full shovel of soil. Not a little namby-pamby hand trowel of the stuff, but a big, deep scoopful, using a real shovel. Ideally,

**If you live in colder climates, make sure you don't use ice salt during the winter near the ground you will be growing food in.**

you want to dig down at least 4–5 inches into the ground. Take a good look at the dirt you've taken out. Are there a lot of rocks in it? Did you hit a tree root as you dug? If you hit one rock or one root, there will definitely be more in that space, and anything that stopped your shovel going straight into the ground will cause you issues going forward. This is important to know as you weigh all the factors before you start. If you didn't hit anything, then I secretly hate you a little right now (I *always* hit something).

Next, take a handful of the dirt (a real handful, not a *glove*ful—you have to make skin contact) and squeeze it tight for 30 seconds. You want to see how well the soil sticks together without moisture (which is why you needed to wait for the 3 days without rain). If the soil doesn't stick together at all but runs through your fingers, you have sand. If the soil sticks together solidly and you can see the perfect outline of your fingers in it, you have clay.

Neither of these situations is ideal. There are lots of websites and blogs about things to add to your sand or clay soil, but *don't listen to them*! Trying to change what you are working with is a total disaster waiting to happen—you may get some short-term success, but in the end the ground will revert to what it originally was, and all the work you did will pretty much be a waste. So if either of these situations is yours, consider going with a raised bed (see page 25) instead of planting directly in the ground, and skip the rest of this section.

The best scenario for your soil is somewhere in between sand and clay, what's called *loam*. This is the sweet spot where part of the dirt clumps and the rest stays loose. Loam is a combination of sand, clay and silt (made up of rock and mineral particles), and generally this combination is what you want for successful planting. It will provide enough water drainage so that the roots won't rot, yet will hold enough moisture that you don't have to be watering multiple times a day.

If you are stressed in any way about the soil in your yard, you can search online to find a soil-testing company near you. Most require you to just send in a simple soil sample, but some of the advanced labs will require a special kit to be sent out to you first. I have a local university test my soil as the reports it produces can be helpful and informative. Be prepared to learn that your soil might not be so good for planting (this is especially likely in urban centers because of all the human activity). Soil with high levels of copper and zinc should definitely be avoided, as your plants will absorb both and pass them on to the food that ends up on your plate.

## Buying Dirt

When it comes to buying dirt, there are generally four types to choose from, and all should be available at most big-box stores or garden centers.

**Garden soil.** An all-purpose mix that will work well in almost any garden bed. Garden soil will often have things added to it like fertilizers or other "plant foods" to help everything grow. You may also find garden soil blends for specific types of plants, which have been specifically mixed to meet a particular plant's needs. While garden soil is a great option for vegetable gardening, make sure to read the label to find out what has been added, because anything in the soil will end up in your food, synthetic fertilizers included.

**Potting soil.** A lighter and looser version of garden soil, designed for planters and container gardening. You will often see little white balls, called *pearlite*, in this mix. These aerate the soil and help to make it lighter (because pearlite is literally lighter than soil, especially wet soil), so this is a good choice for pots, planters and vertical gardens. You may also see the term *vermiculite* printed on the potting-mix bag. Vermiculite is an additive that helps water and nutrient retention in the soil, for healthier plants. Like pearlite, it is great for vertical gardens and containers because it is lightweight. Many store-bought soils will contain both pearlite and vermiculite in the mixes. These are great options for the first-time gardener but can be pricier because of the "extras" inside.

**Topsoil.** This is soil that has literally been scraped off the ground. Perfect name for it, don't you think? Topsoil has nothing added to it, no nutrients or fertilizers, so it's nothing but what is already in the ground. For in-ground gardening, I generally use bagged topsoil as my base and then mix it with compost or manure. This is a cheaper option to some of the expensive premixed soils out there.

**Triple mix.** Three soils in one bag! A winner for the vegetable grower! Triple mix usually includes an all-purpose topsoil, along with peat moss to help hold moisture and either a compost or manure to increase plant growth. I use triple mix exclusively in all my raised beds because it has everything my vegetables need to grow.

# UNDERSTANDING YOUR SPACE

T here are many ways to plant, and some obvious and not so obvious things to look for when planning what kind of garden will work for you. So take a look at your space and the chart (on pages 42–43) showing the different types of gardens and planting options available to you.

## In-Ground Gardens

My grandma always planted her vegetable garden directly in the ground. For her, and generations before her, planting directly in the ground was the go-to, and it's now the dream for many of us. In-ground is cheaper than paying for raised beds or containers. If you have good dirt and lots of sun, then all you'll need are seeds + water + hard labor, and you get great food for very little money.

Whether you are starting a new in-ground garden from scratch, or planning to resurrect an old one or convert an existing lawn, the steps for in-ground gardening are basically the same—and the goal is most definitely the same: getting the dirt in top-notch condition before you begin.

### Turning Existing Dirt into a Vegetable Garden

If you are working with existing ground, you have to prep the soil well before planting. Basically, that means removing all existing grass and weeds so that you can start afresh when planting new stuff. If you don't get absolutely everything out of there, they will for sure grow back. Here's the deal, though: Grass usually has roots that are 4–6 inches deep, and for weeds they can go up to 12 inches. Which means the success of your planting totally depends on how anal you are about getting rid of absolutely all the roots. There are a few ways to tackle the job—I've laid them out below, so you can decide what works best for you.

### Rip It Out

Whether you go all Neanderthal and start ripping weeds out by hand, or you stick a shovel in the ground and start digging, you are basically ripping the stuff out. Seriously, that's it. If you have a lawn that you want to grow food in and don't have a lot of money, just start digging! Make sure you have a lot of painkillers on hand though (or get some CrossFit training in first) because this is seriously hard work.

On the plus side, once you get started, you can dig out and prepare your plot pretty quickly. Just keep digging, never going deeper than you have to, until all the grass and weeds are removed from the section you want to plant in. The blade length of a full-sized garden shovel is about as deep as the roots of your lawn will be growing. If you are leaving some of the existing lawn in place, then you might find you're creating a bit of a pit for your vegetable garden that sits below the level of the rest of the lawn. This is a good thing, though, because rainwater will naturally funnel into this lower space during the hot, dry months of summer, keeping your garden well hydrated. If you are worried about the cat falling in, buy bags of garden soil to pour overtop, filling the pit to a level you're comfortable with.

**A word of warning: Before you start using any machinery in your yard, make sure you call your utility providers and have your utility lines located. There are things to watch out for—like the cable wires and gas lines!—and you should never assume that everything is located at the front of your house (and yes, I'm totally speaking from experience here).**

### Rototiller That Shit

If the idea of digging out the space by hand sounds too brutal, consider using a rototiller instead. You can rent this little beast from almost any big-box store or borrow it from

any hard-core gardeners on your street. Using a rototiller takes all the digging out of the process, because the machine chops up the clumps of soil and grass into manageable sections that you can then remove piece by piece. This is way easier than using a shovel. Keep in mind that because you're chopping up the grass and the weeds, you will have lots of little roots chopped up and spread about. Every one of those little roots has the potential to turn into a weed, so you need to get rid of them—all of them—even the ones under the ground, which you can't initially see.

## Lasagna Gardening

If everything you've read so far sounds like a lot of work, you might try my favorite method instead: lasagna gardening. Sounds tasty, right? The best part is that you can lasagna-garden pretty much anywhere there is soil, including on top of an old or existing garden, or your lawn. You will need to plan early with this method, though, as it takes about 6 months for the space to be ready for you to start planting in.

A lasagna garden uses layers of cardboard, newspapers and mulch as a barrier to block the sun and stop the grass and weeds from continuing to grow underneath. Basically, you are killing all the unwanted plants by smothering them with mulch and cardboard (rather than you having to rip everything out). When it's time to garden, you move aside the cardboard and plant directly into the dirt below.

# Lasagna Garden

**1**

Start by collecting recycled cardboard and newspaper, avoiding anything with a glossy finish (those don't naturally break down). Don't worry if your boxes are covered in print—the ink is soy-based and non-toxic. Remove any tape and staples and flatten any boxes.

**2**

Pick the spot where you want your veggie garden to be, and place the cardboard on top of the ground in that area. Put down the cardboard first and then tuck newspaper under the edges, or anywhere there is soil showing through. Your goal is to have absolutely no ground exposed, so there are absolutely no spots for weeds to grow. If you're working in a tight spot or around existing plants, use only newspaper instead of cardboard because it is more flexible. About 7 layers of newspaper should do it.

**3**

Bury the cardboard and newspaper in at least 3 inches of mulch (available at any garden center or big-box store). Mulch can be in the form of wood chips, compost or even decaying leaves. Lightly spray the entire area with water to "glue" it all together and help keep the mulch from moving.

**4**

It takes a while for the "lasagna" layers to break down and kill the weeds below, so you need to be patient. Give it at least 6 months before digging into the ground to see if anything is still growing. If the ground is clear, you're good to go! If there is still some grass or weeds, either rip them out or redo a layer of the paper mulch combination and keep waiting.

**5**

When it's time to start planting, remove the mulch from the spot you want to plant in, make a hole in whatever cardboard is left underneath and plant directly in the soil below. You can leave the remaining mulch-covered cardboard in between what you are planting: It is made of natural fibers and will continue to break down over time, adding nutrients to the soil and preventing any new weeds from growing in the meantime.

**6**

If weeds start to build up again, repeat the process. If you'd rather create a weed-free patio or walkway, swap the mulch for pea gravel.

# Raised Beds and Planter Boxes

In the most simplistic terms, a *raised bed* is four walls that create a box, that is then filled with a lot of soil. Because they have no bottom, raised beds are usually placed directly on top of the ground, so the water drains right into the ground below. A *planter box* is pretty much the same thing as a raised bed but with a bottom, so it can be used on a patio or balcony, or anywhere really that you have space (I've seen them on the sidewalk in front of people's houses before). Raised beds and planter boxes are my favorite garden spaces for lots of reasons. The most obvious may be that because they are raised off the ground, you don't have to bend over as much. (Which people of any age will be grateful for!)

But they have several other advantages too. Number one is that they allow you to garden in the soil of your choosing. By working on top of the existing ground, a raised bed lets you garden in a space where the soil is crappy. Whether you have rock, clay or even sketchy soil, building a bed or a box on top of it and adding the soil of your choosing means that your plants have the best chance to grow big and healthy.

They're also very adaptable. Most vegetables only need 4–8 inches of soil to grow, and this means that, with enough height, you can build a planter box on top of gravel or even concrete. Just remember that when you water it, the soil may run out the gaps between the boards if you don't line it properly first (more about this on page 29).

If space allows, having multiple raised beds/planters will also help you rotate your plants. Like a farmer, if you want your vegetable garden to last a long time, you will have to rotate your crops (see Companion Planting on page 60).

Different plants have different needs when it comes to minerals in soil, and as they grow, they take from the soil what they need if it's available to them. If you move your plants around between the raised beds/planters, you will help ensure that one spot of soil isn't drained of all its nutrients.

Raised beds and planters are also useful at deterring several kinds of pests, including bunnies (evil bunnies!). By elevating your garden and building walls around it, you will slow down a lot of things that want to eat your plants. Only the bravest of rabbits will jump up onto an 18-inch-high garden, where they will be so exposed. Raised beds/planters will also protect your plants from dogs that like to tear around the yard at max speed and trash plants at will. It's much easier to teach dogs not to jump into the raised garden than it is to get them to stay out of a ground-level bed.

**DIY**

# Raised Beds & Planter Boxes

Building a planter box or raised bed is not hard. Think planks of wood with corner supports and you've already worked out most of what you'll need to do!

## Wood Choices

The wood you use is a big deal. Wood is porous, so anything that is on it will eventually leach into your garden and get into your veggies. A clean wood (one that doesn't contain any preservatives or chemicals) that can handle moisture is your best bet. Another good option is lumber with an environmental approval showing that the treatments used are either safe or will not leach into the soil. There are many types of wood available, but the three most common options are:

### Cedar.

Often considered the best choice as well as one of the most expensive. On average, cedar will last 20-plus years in the garden. It is a "clean" wood because it's not treated with any preservatives, but it can be difficult to find because it's so popular.

### Pressure-treated.

This is a blend of woods that have been chemically treated to withstand the elements. New technology is changing the types of preservatives used and reducing the amount of chemicals that leach into the soil, making this a relatively environmentally friendly choice. It's readily available at low prices.

### Redwood.

Probably the nicest looking of the three options, with a beautiful natural color. Redwood will last as long as cedar in the garden, but since it's harvested from a limited supply of trees, it's the most expensive of the options.

## Size Matters

The width of the raised bed/planter is really important: Keep it 4 feet max. You need to be able to care for your plants, and to do this you have to be able to reach them. I'm six-foot-five, and even with my long arms I have a hard time getting to the center of a raised bed/planter that is 5 feet wide. The average person can comfortably reach 2 feet away when bending over, which makes 4 feet the limit. If you are building up against a wall, keep to under 2 feet, since you won't be able to get to the plants from all sides.

*(continued)*

For height, go to a maximum of 18 inches. This is the magic number for easily dumping soil over the sides of the walls. Remember: the higher the raised bed/planter, the more soil you'll need to fill it. I built mine knowing that each raised bed/planter would need about 30 wheelbarrows full of soil. In the end, I hauled 750 wheelbarrows of soil to fill my beds. (Best leg day EVER!)

## Raised Bed

### Materials

- 100 pack 2½-inch outdoor screws (you'll use 50–60 of the screws)
- 4 or 6 wood boards cut to the length of your desired planter (8 feet is good, see below)
- 4 or 6 wood boards cut to width of your planter (4 feet max, see page 27 for best wood choices)
- 4 wood posts, 4 × 4 inches each, cut to the height of your planter (18 inches max, see below)
- For planters longer than 6 feet: 2 wood braces (2- × 8–12-inch wide boards, cut to the height of the planter). Any type of wood works for these.

1. First, decide where your raised bed is going to go. Ideally, you'll be able to access it from all sides, to maximize how you can use it, so think long and hard before building one up against a wall.

2. Level out the ground that it will sit on as much as possible. If you build the bed on an uneven section of lawn, soil will leak out the bottom every time you water it (unless you line it with landscape fabric). Also, every time someone like me comes to visit, you'll have to hear that your bed isn't level. (Just sayin'.)

3. Cover the ground under the bottom of your raised planter with either cardboard or newspaper to help stop any weeds that are already in the ground from growing up into your new beds.

4. Lay out the first level of boards in your bed's shape—make a flat rectangle with all four sides lying on the ground. You should have 2 lengthwise boards and 2 width-wise boards. Next, place a 4- × 4-inch post in each corner. Flip each of the boards onto their sides and anchor them to the posts. If you try to attach the boards together without the corner supports, the weight of the soil will start to pull the

boards apart over time. I like to attach them using outdoor screws instead of nails so that they hold together longer.

5. Once you've got the first set of boards in place, repeat the process and screw the next set of the lengthwise boards on top of the first. Repeat until you have reached your desired height.

6. If your planter is longer than 6 feet, you'll need to add a vertical wooden brace to the inside of it to stop the sides from bowing out from the weight of the soil. Screw a vertical board in the center of each of the two long sides of the planter. These braces will hold the boards together and are hidden once you add the soil.

7. Line the bottom and sides of the bed with landscape fabric (geotextile) to prevent soil from leaking out of the bottom. Staple the fabric to the inside of the boards. This will never be seen, so don't worry too much about making it tidy; just bring the fabric high enough up the sides so that the soil will be able to hold it in place.

8. Fill the bed with soil. Try to keep the soil light and fluffy—compacted soil will be harder for your plants and seeds to grow in.

9. If your bed is bowing out in the middle once full, attach a wooden brace (see step 6) to the outside of the planter for extra support. It doesn't look pretty, but it's worth it!

## Planter Box

### Materials
Same as Raised Bed (see page 28), but you need enough additional wood boards cut to the length of your desired planter to form the bottom of the box (the number will depend on the width of your planter).

1. Follow the steps for building a Raised Bed (see pages 28–29) until after step 6.

2. Attach the additional boards across the bottom of the box to form the base. If you want feet on your planter to raise it up off the ground, go ahead and attach those now. Once all that is in place, flip the planter over so it's sitting on the base (or feet, if you added them). Then, continue with steps 7–9.

# Bag Gardens

Bag gardens have been circling the bowl for a few years now. The theory behind them is that you cut out the center of a bag of soil and plant your vegetables directly inside. Easy, right? Will it work? Of course! Plants are very forgiving—even if you grow them in a bag.

1. Pick a section of your lawn or a weedy garden bed, and rake and level it.

2. Place the bag of soil upside down beside its final destination.

3. Slice two big cuts through the bottom of the bag (these are drainage slits) and then gently roll the bag over and into place. Do not lift the bag after you've sliced it or the soil will end up everywhere.

4. Cut out a large section of plastic from the center of the top of the bag, leaving the sides intact.

5. Plant in the bag.

So easy, and yet . . . I wouldn't do it! Surprised? Here are the problems I see with this method:

**Drainage.** This is the first big issue. Although the plants will take root, water will still collect in the bottom of the bag, even with the drainage slits, and the soil will become saturated. Plants such as tomatoes and basil hate to have wet feet. And if you do put lots of holes in the bottom, every time you water your garden the soil will leak out, leaving less for the plants.

**Space.** Where to put the bag garden? If you put the bags on the lawn, they'll smother any plants growing underneath them (although this may not be a bad thing if you want to use that space later as an in-ground garden). If you put the bags on concrete, the soil and water leaking out of the bag will cause some serious staining (making this a definite non-option for patios).

**Staking.** Be prepared to stake your bags. Larger vegetable plants like tomatoes, peppers and corn grow much bigger than their anchoring root system and often need additional support to handle the weight of the plant. With limited depth in your bag garden, things will start to fall over pretty quickly.

**Cleaning.** At the end of the year, this will also be no fun. The bags with the split on the top and the holes in the bottom won't transport easily—an issue especially if you are planning to do the right thing and compost the roots and spent plants. You will have to cut open each bag completely, strip the plastic from the soil and then try to remove the mess. Good luck with that.

**Attractiveness.** Who the hell wants to look at plastic bags in their backyard all summer? And no amount of mulch will make bag gardens look good.

Let's just call this idea a total *#gardenfail* waiting to happen.

# Straw Bale Gardens

The *straw bale garden* is a "love it or hate it" type of garden for most homeowners. It's a simple concept: Put plants in a straw bale and let them root in the natural pockets created by the dried grass. As the straw breaks down and decomposes, your garden is fertilized. It's a little more complicated than that, but you get the gist. There are definitely big pluses with a straw bale garden:

- They are built on top of the ground and can be installed on any surface, including hills, decks and patios.
- They don't need much soil compared with a raised bed because you are planting in the straw.
- The bales fertilize your garden as they break down and can be composted afterward, to provide more nutrients to plants in later years.
- The usual garden pests don't know what to do with straw bales. Dirt they get, but straw? Not so much. So your plants have a better fighting chance as a result.

Sounds great, right? But there are a few cons as well that you should know about:

- Straw bales are messy, and not just a little messy, but *seriously* messy. That straw spreads everywhere while you're setting it up and continues to do so every time it gets a little windy.
- Straw bales, as they break down, have a distinct funk. You'd have to put them down-wind and pray that the breeze keeps the musky odor away from your sitting area.

- For straw bales to work best, you want them to rot and be covered in beneficial mold and fungus. Enough said.
- Mice and little creatures love to live in straw bales, so unless you are Snow White and want a woodland family, be prepared for some unwanted guests.
- You have to deal with the straw bales even after the garden is done. That means a big ol' pile of fermenting straw sitting in your space until it completely decomposes.
- Square straw bales are a bitch to find. Farmers don't make them as much anymore because they now use bigger ones to feed the herds. Hard to find = expensive.

# Straw Bale Garden

In case you haven't figured it out already, let me tell you that there won't be a straw bale garden in my near future! But if you still want one, the good news is that they're super easy to build:

**Grow in rows.** With straw bales, this will make life simpler. Start with a row of bales turned on their sides so that the tips of the straw are pointing up and down.

**Secure the bales.** You need to fasten these bales down so they don't tip over. If you have ground underneath them, just hammer some spikes through the bale and into the soil below. If you are on a deck or a patio, make the row two bales thick and tie all the bales together for extra stability, using a heavy-duty natural hemp rope or twine.

**Soak the bales.** We're not talking a little water here; these bales need to be kept *very, very* wet to kick-start the natural process of decomposition. Seasoned straw bale gardeners will put a drip hose on top of the bale so that the constant watering is even.

**Plant in the bales.** If you are putting in veggies like tomatoes and peppers that are already a plant, simply make a hole in the straw and stick them in. If you want to grow from seeds, put 1–2 inches of soil on top of the bales and plant your seeds in that. They will root into the straw below.

**Maintain the bales.** Even carrots and root vegetables can grow in straw so long as it is kept very wet. As soon as those bales dry out (because you went camping for the weekend, say) the project is done, so make sure you stay on top of watering.

# Container Gardens

Personally, I think containers are the perfect solution for growing vegetables in any space . . . just put them in a pot! There are very few veggies that won't grow in a decent-sized pot, so if you have a limited space with no direct access to the ground, this is totally the solution for you. You might be surprised at how rewarding container gardening can be.

**Versatile.** You can move them easily around your space, whether you're chasing the sun or just changing up your garden's decor. Ultimately, they are excellent void fillers. They are the perfect solution for filling empty spots around the outside of your home. I put containers on decks, patios and balconies, and even directly in the garden.

**Awesome visual impact.** Containers can be a real focal point in your space. How much impact they create is up to you. If you want your container to immediately draw the eye, use bright-colored plants in a sunny location (deep-red lettuces or bright-yellow zucchini flowers pop in the sunshine). If you want something a little less obvious, you might go for green leaves—lots of them in the shade are amazing at creating understated elegance. Consider the color of the container you are working with. Bright-colored planters tend to draw the eye away from what is inside. This can work in your favor if you are looking for a pop of color in your space and everything you have planted is the same shade of green.

**Any size you want.** Containers range from small pots holding only one plant to big ones acting as mini veggie gardens with multiple varieties. Never be afraid of going big with a planter. Lately, I've been putting large planters in small spaces; I love the drama they create. I am also a fan of creating different visual planes with plants. Too often we think of gardening as starting on the ground and building up from there, but with planters you can start at whatever height you want—just choose the planter accordingly. This is really helpful on a balcony or rooftop if you need to create some privacy from your neighbors. Just get planters that are the right height to hide you from the world when you are sitting at your bistro table.

**Mix 'n' match plants.** There is absolutely no reason you can't grow beans and lilies in the same pot! And by pairing flowers with your vegetables, you increase the number of pollinators (like bees) that will be attracted to your space, which will in turn give you more veggies.

# Vertical Garden

Sometimes the only choice for a vegetable garden is up! Vertical gardening is the perfect option for many condo and apartment dwellers because of limited patio or balcony space. And the good news is that vegetables will grow in pretty much anything (including pallets, red Solo cups, eavestroughs mounted on a wall . . .). You'll need to address a few challenges before you start drilling holes in a wall though:

**Gardening is messy.** Vertical gardening is perhaps messiest of all because the soil is suspended off the ground. Every time you water your garden or it rains, the soil will try to find its way back to the ground, potentially leaving mud smears and stains all over the walls and concrete below. Consider painting the wall beforehand with a washable paint or concrete sealer.

**Soil is heavy.** You need to account for the weight of the wet soil when mounting a vertical garden. Too often, people will build something really cool, mount it on the wall, add soil and plants—and then have the whole thing come down because of the weight. (Goodbye, garden. Hello, big holes in the wall.)

**Weather matters.** It can be windy up high, and most veggies can't do wind. So consider putting your vertical garden on a wall that provides some shelter but where it will still get lots of sun.

Although DIY-ing your vertical garden is doable and will save you money, I'm a big fan of using premade versions. Most have been designed to deal with the water-and-mud issue just mentioned, and come with proper screws and mounting brackets to handle the weight of the garden. If you want your garden to be an art piece as well as functional, add flowers and herbs in with the veggies. Also consider using trailing or vine veggies like mini cucumbers, peas, beans and dwarf zucchini. The best veggies for a vertical garden? Pretty much all of them! The only one I wouldn't try growing on a wall is corn, but I'm sure someone somewhere has done it. Even small versions of our favorite root vegetables will grow on a wall—check out Paris Round carrots!

Remember, bugs and birds will visit your splash of green no matter where you are, even a condo balcony high in the sky—don't freak out if bees or birds start to build a nest in your small space. Nature happens everywhere!

## Window Gardens

Using exterior window boxes is a classic way to grow plants in crowded city spaces where there are no patios and balconies. The rules for the other types of gardens apply here too, just on a smaller scale. Make sure to test for light levels. And choose a planter with good drainage, for when the water overflows. I prefer options that drain away from the wall, so that you don't get streaking down the side of the building from the mud (look for planters that have the hole in the middle of the bottom instead of ones that have drainage holes along the outside edges). When choosing plants for your veggie window box, choose ones that grow vertically, as opposed to vines, which will hang down unless supported by a trellis. Reaching your cucumbers or beans when they are hanging 5 feet below your window is tricky unless you have climbing gear!

## Community Garden

No outdoor space at all? No problem! Even though you can grow some tasty and healthy edibles indoors, you might want to consider joining a local community garden or co-op. I love this option for newbie gardeners because you'll be surrounded by a whole group of experts, and odds are that one of them will be willing to offer you advice if you get into trouble. Once you have your plot secured, turn back to pages 9 and 14 to refresh yourself on how to assess the sunlight and soil, and then to page 19 for tips on how to prepare the ground. And keep in mind the rules of etiquette when it comes to growing vegetables with others:

**Never ask to try another gardener's food.** If they offer you a bean or a carrot, then it's fair game, but asking to sample someone else's crop is kind of a no-no unless you are prepared to trade with something from your own garden.

**Never plant invasive species.** Plants like mint should be avoided in your plot unless you have a way to control the spread. The worst part of community gardening is dealing with someone else's garden sprawl. Do your best to contain the plants in your own space. The trellises and fences don't have to be pretty—they just have to work and not obstruct anyone else. Sometimes your neighbor will plant something tall like sunflowers or corn, which will block some of the sunlight to your garden for part of the day. Don't stress—the sun is always moving and your plants will still get plenty of light.

**Follow through.** If you commit to caring for a garden plot, you need to care for it for the entire season. No quitting halfway through the year because it's too hot outside.

**Go *au naturel.*** Beware of using herbicides, pesticides or insecticides. Almost all community gardens are chemical-free. Look to natural options for solving your pest and insect problems.

**Stay on top of things.** Avoid letting your food start to rot, even if rotting vegetables are a great addition to the compost pile. And even if the smell deters the local rodent population, it won't work so well for your neighbors.

# CHOOSING THE RIGHT GARDEN FOR YOU

| GARDEN TYPE | Backyard | Front Yard |
|---|---|---|
| **In-Ground (page 19)** | Of course! Gardening in the ground of your own backyard is the dream for most people growing food. | Definitely possible but check local bylaws and condo rules first. |
| **Raised Beds / Planter Boxes (page 25)** | For sure! These can be designed and built to fit any space. | Of course! |
| **Bag (page 30)** | The backyard is the only spot for one of these. | X |
| **Straw Bale (page 31)** | If you really have to, then in the back is best. | X |
| **Container (page 35)** | Yes, please. I love using pots on the edge of a deck. | Just make sure they aren't going to get swiped! |
| **Vertical (page 39)** | Something to try on a garden wall, or maybe your fence? | Probably not, but you'll have to be the judge of your space. |
| **Community (page 40)** | X | X |

| Patio | Balcony/ Rooftop | Windowsill | No Outdoor Space Whatsoever |
|---|---|---|---|
| Some patios have planting pockets built in. Tricky to work with but not impossible. | X | X | See Community Garden below! |
| Absolutely! | Sure! Just make sure to keep any soil or muddy water from raining on your neighbors below. | It needs to be a really big sill. | See Community Garden below! |
| X | X | X | X |
| X | X | X | X |
| 100 percent! This is my favorite way to make the most of patio space. | Yes, please! | The best way to go for a window garden | See Community Garden below! |
| Any wall can work! | Definitely! | Maybe on the wall inside the windowsill . . . | You could buy an indoor-friendly version (but never DIY because they always leak). |
| X | X | X | This is the place for you! Here is where you can try your hand at in-ground gardening, planter boxes or containers, whatever works best. |

# ALL YOU NEED FOR SEED

**A**lthough baby plants, called *seedlings*, are pretty easy to buy at the garden centers, when you grow from seed it is a lot cheaper, and you also have a lot more variety to choose from. A garden center may carry 20 or even 50 types of seedling tomatoes, but would you believe there are over 10,000 varieties of seeds available through online seed suppliers?!

## When to Start?

Different regions have different magical "planting dates" to tell you when you should start to plant your seeds outdoors. That planting date is calculated forward from the last frost. Promise me that, as enthusiastic as you are, you won't get suckered into starting early—if the weather isn't right or you get a frost, I'm telling you your plants will suffer. I've been burned so many times, and it's not worth it—the guilt of freezing all those baby plants is something you just won't forget.

In North America, there is a spread of 3 months during which our planting dates fall, and they are different, of course, in different regions, due to the different climates we have across the continent. For example, gardeners in Vancouver and Seattle can start planting around March 28, but if you're on the east coast, you'll need to wait until May 15. In the middle of the continent, May 24 is the typical ballpark date, whereas June 1 is common in mountainous areas. To get an accurate planting date for your specific region, it's best to look it up online; or ask your neighbor if they seem to know what they're doing! Once you know this you are ready to roll.

## Starting Indoors

My first time ordering seeds, I missed the little phrase on the back of several packages: "Start indoors." It really does mean that you have to start growing the seeds indoors (in a protected place with lots of light, see page 49 for more info). The seed package has a lot of info on it that you need to understand before you begin planting. This is not info to skip over as it will help you avoid *#gardenfails* for sure, so make sure you read it thoroughly before tossing! Some seeds need to be started indoors a full 12 weeks before they are transferred to the garden outside. This is where many new seed growers fail. Certain plants, including peppers, tomatoes and eggplants, benefit from a good head start inside, because they need lots of time to produce lots of fruit. So once you know your magical planting date, count backward on the calendar to determine the date to start indoors. This table tells you how early to plant the seeds of popular veggies:

| Vegetable | Weeks Before Planting Date |
|---|---|
| Onions | 10–12 |
| Peppers | 8–10 |
| Cabbage | 6–8 |
| Cauliflower | 6–8 |
| Tomatoes | 6–8 |
| Broccoli | 4–6 |
| Head Lettuce | 4–6 |
| Cucumbers | 4 |

## Maturity Date

Before you plant any seeds, pay close attention to the *maturity date*—the length of time it will take the plant to start to produce a harvest. In northern areas, beware of plants that need more than 95 days because the time between your spring thaw and winter freeze won't be long enough to get a crop. I tried to grow an amazing Japanese eggplant last year, and although the plant was healthy and I got fruit started, our first frost came early and I ended up with mush ... *#gardenfail* (although technically it was a *#seedfail*)!

The term *growing season* refers to the time between the last frost of the year and the first frost in the fall.

The farther south you go, the longer the growing season. This is important to know when considering a plant's maturity date (see page 45). If the maturity date is longer than the growing season of your area, you will have to start your seeds indoors.

Depending on your timing, it might be easier to start with seed varieties that are labeled on the package as *direct sow*. These seeds are planted directly in the garden, so don't have to be started indoors first. These plants are fast growers and don't need extra time to produce a harvest. Radishes are a perfect example: They mature fast enough that you can grow a crop, harvest them and grow another round in the same spot, all within one summer.

# Best Seeds to Buy?

Seeds seem to be available absolutely everywhere—online, at garden centers, even at your local corner store. But before you run off to source much-hyped heirloom seeds to grow in your garden, let me explain a few terms that will help you avoid the potholes of seed buying.

## Seed Definitions

**GMO.** These are plants that have been genetically modified. The crosses between species are done in a lab, very differently from the hybrid varieties (see below). GMOs are created on a cellular level by messing around with the DNA of the species and adding genes that would never actually exist in nature. While a lot of good things can be done with this technology, many people in the growing community are very aware that playing God may have negative implications—creating plants that don't naturally exist in nature may have long-term impacts that we can't even imagine yet. There has been a lot of speculation about disease-resistant invasive plants that can destroy a natural ecosystem because they have been modified to withstand everything.

**Heirloom.** This term is tossed around a lot, but cleanly put, heirloom seeds are those of plant varieties that are at least 50 years old. We used to say that they needed to have been passed down from family to family, but some commercial seed types have now been around since the 1940s, so many of them are considered heirlooms as well. A lot of growers research the strains of their plants and can track them back centuries.

**Hybrid.** This refers to the types of veggies created by plant breeders, who cross two specific plants in an attempt to achieve particular traits in the offspring. Almost all the options that are labeled "new" types of tomatoes and peppers are crossed using this method. It's sort of like being set up on a blind date and being told the two of you should have kids because you both have beautiful blue eyes. Although these plants are man-made(ish), they are

**You might consider using a seed-starting kit, readily available at garden centers or online. These kits usually include a set of good-sized containers, a tray to set them on and a clear lid to hold in humidity during the early stages.**

considered natural because the breeders use the plants' own reproductive systems to propagate them.

**Open-pollinated.** These are seeds from plants that are pollinated by nature—bees, butterflies or wind—and produce plants that often have the same traits year after year. They are considered more genetically diverse, as each season a different source pollinates them. These plants are often better suited to their growing conditions than others because they have naturally evolved and adapted in that space. For example, if you plant the same tomato plant in the same garden year after year (using the seeds you collected from that plant the year before), the plant will strengthen with its adaptation to the space (and, bonus, the tomatoes will start to taste better over time!).

## Preparing to Seed

Once you've picked your seeds and figured out your timing, there are a few more things you should know. For a plant to grow from a seed, it will need light, oxygen, something to grow in, a growing medium (dirt!) and water. While this may sound simple, it's easy to make mistakes along the way, and I know firsthand that even a little mistake can mean having to start at the very beginning all over again.

**Light.** Seeds need at least 12–14 hours of intense light per day. A south-facing window providing southern exposure always works (provided that a large building isn't blocking your sunlight), but most gardeners go with a DIY growing system, using artificial light and a timer (see below). A growing system like this allows you to control the height of the light, helping your seedlings grow straight and tall but not leggy. (*Leggy* means weak and skinny; leggy is good only for supermodels.)

**DIY**

# Growing System

You can make your own growing system with things you have around the house.
Basically, it all comes down to the light. Seed starting indoors is done with a full-spectrum light bulb that covers all the light levels found in nature. Here's how to build your own system:

### Materials
- 1 wire shelving or rack unit with adjustable shelf heights
- 1 plastic boot tray (designed for holding wet boots) that will fit in the shelving unit. This is to help contain the water that may leak out of any pots.
- 1- × 4-inch shop-light fixture (available at any garden center or big-box store)
- Full-spectrum light tubes that fit your light fixture—1 or 2 should provide plenty of light
- 1 electric or digital timer

1. Mount the light fixture on the underside of the top shelf of the shelving unit. Most light fixtures come with a built-in mounting system, or use chain or zip ties.

2. Place the second shelf 10 inches below the light and put the boot tray on it.

3. Plant your seeds in a container or device with drainage holes (see Containers, page 50).

4. As the seeds begin to sprout from the soil, lower the shelf, maintaining a distance of 6–10 inches between it and the light, for high-intensity light. If the top leaves of the seedlings are turning brown and crispy, lower the shelf even more.

5. Plug the light fixture into the timer and set it to provide your seedlings with 18 hours of light per day. You can keep your plants growing this way all season long, or you can transplant them outside once the warm weather has arrived.

**Don't start with too big a container—the roots of vegetables need soil only 3–4 inches deep to grow. A large container means a lot of unused soil.**

**Containers.** Anything that will hold the soil and let you get the plant out easily once it grows will work as a container. Pretty much anything in the recycling bin is fair game. I've seen people use eggshells (with the top portion cut off), but they seem a little fragile to me. Don't start with too big a container—the roots of vegetables need soil only 3–4 inches deep to grow. A large container means a lot of unused soil.

**Growing medium.** Growing from seeds can be tricky, as baby plants are fragile. I use a seed-starting soil mix that is light and fluffy. I prefer to use mixes that have a vermiculite component (it looks like little white confetti), which holds moisture. Don't worry about adding fertilizer, as bagged seed-starting mixes are ready to use.

**Water.** Plants, like people, are made mostly of water, so they definitely need lots of it to grow. I prefer to water from the bottom because otherwise I am often cursed with fungus growing on the top of the soil, which will kill the seedlings as they try to grow. To water from the bottom, place your plant containers on a shallow tray (or, my favorite, a boot tray) and pour small amounts of water into the tray, a bit at a time, watching to see that it is absorbed into the soil through the container's drainage holes.

To start seeds, keep the soil moist but not saturated. As the seeds grow and turn into seedlings, reduce the frequency of watering so that the top of the soil dries out just a little. Be careful to give your plants only what they can absorb. Allow the top of the soil to dry out between waterings, otherwise your plant roots will get waterlogged and potentially drown.

# How to Plant Seeds

1. Start by choosing a container that has a hole in the bottom for excess water to drain out, and sometimes for moisture to be absorbed from below when you need to add it.

2. Fill the container with a soil designed for seed starting. (I keep my soil in a big bin and then fill my pots by dipping them in it, to keep everything nice and clean.)

3. Seeds all like to be planted at different depths so read the package before you start. The rule of thumb is that the depth of the hole should be twice the size of the seed. If the package says the seeds "need light," simply place them on top of the soil. When planting into the soil, I usually use the bottom of a pencil or a pen to make a small hole and then drop the seed into it. Then I gently cover the seed with some soil from the sides.

4. I prefer to always water my seeds from the bottom by placing my pots/containers in a second tray that will hold at least 1 inch of water. If you decide to water from the top, make sure to remember that the first time you water, add just a touch, so that the soil can absorb it without the seeds being washed away. Once the plants get started, they will develop roots, which will help hold them in place, and then you can be a little more liberal with the watering.

5. Label your seeds immediately so you can keep track of what you're growing and where. I almost always forget and then am screwed until the plant grows fruit.

6. Your seeds (now seedlings) are ready to be transplanted into either the garden or larger containers when they have grown strong and tall with a good root system in place. I usually aim for 4–6 inches tall for my peppers and tomatoes. You can check their root system by gently working the plant out of the starting container by squeezing it up from the bottom. You want plants with lots of roots because they are generally stronger than ones with only a couple. The roots allow them more access to nutrients and water in the soil.

### Seed Starting Kit

You might consider a seed starting kit, readily available at garden centers or online. These kits usually include a set of good-sized containers, a tray to set them on and a clear lid to hold in humidity during the early stages. Just make sure to remove the lids once the seeds sprout, so that no fungus grows on the soil.

## Moving Outdoors

Whether your plants were grown from seed or purchased as seedlings from a garden center, they need time to adjust to the outdoors before being planted in the ground.

Plants, like pale people, need to get used to full sun before they can be outside all day long. Start by bringing out your plant babies in their existing containers for 20 minutes on the first day, then 40 minutes on the second and then 60 minutes on the third. After that, you are good to plant them into the garden or permanent containers. I recommend this approach for store-bought seedlings that were indoors as well—you don't know how much direct sunlight they have had before you got them.

# PLANNING PRIMER

**January.** Start laying out your garden plans now. Count your pots and planters, and order your seeds. I'm a huge fan of ordering vegetable seeds online. Sitting indoors during the cold winter months in your sweats or pajamas, planning for a spring garden, is a fantastic way to spend a Saturday.

**February.** Set up your indoor grow op. Get the lights ready; purchase the seed-starting soil and planting trays. Also save all those take-out containers to use as trays for growing onions, which can be started at the end of this month. In addition to your onions and shallots, you can start any perennial flowers you are growing from seeds, things like daylilies and poppies.

**March.** You should now be full swing into your seed growing. Everything needs to start hitting the soil now, so that when the warm weather begins, you are ready to get your babies outside and into the sun.

**April.** Some lucky gardeners can start gardening outdoors now because they already have warm weather. If you are in a warm climate, start planting seeds outdoors and moving your indoor seedlings outside—just make sure to get them outdoor-ready first (see Moving Outdoors, page 52). For the rest of us, April is the time to transplant seedlings into larger temporary containers (like red Solo cups). This is also the time to increase the light levels for your indoor plants to support their growth, which helps prevent them from getting too spindly or leggy (see page 49).

**May.** Ready, set, grow! All the plants should be outside in May. Seeds can also be sown for anything you didn't start indoors. Once everything is neatly put into the ground and labeled (see page 63), add a light cover of mulch to help hold in moisture and prevent weed seeds from getting established.

**June.** The first radishes and lettuces should be ready to eat! All your early crops are maturing enough that you can begin to harvest and make those first salads of summer... and nothing has ever tasted so sweet! June is also all about the weeding. The more of the unwanted plants you can get out of the ground now, the less competition your vegetables will have for nutrients and water later.

**July.** The garden is in full swing with beans, peas, carrots and tomatoes... everything you have been working on since January! Planters on the balcony are brimming and the vertical wall is full of fresh greens. July is the happiest month in the garden, as the ground is still moist from spring rains and the sun is at its brightest. Now is the time to get into insect-prevention mode (if you haven't already). Also start collecting rainwater and any other sources of moisture to help with the drier months ahead.

**August.** Bring on the heat! Traditionally one of the warmest months, August is all about water management and harvesting everything that can't handle the heat. Keep an eye on your broccoli and leafy greens like spinach—the heat brings out the worst in both. August is also the time to start collecting seeds for next year.

**September.** With cooler nights, it's time to start thinking about putting the garden to bed—but don't do that before you plant a few extra rows of cold-weather plants like beets and carrots. This is when I begin drying my herbs and making preserves (see page 170). September is the perfect month for hitting the farmers markets, to offset anything you didn't grow in your own space. This is also the month to start a lasagna garden for next year (see page 22).

**October.** Get your garden cleanup in full swing. Make sure to empty all those planters on the balcony and clean up the vertical wall. If they freeze with a blast of cold at the end of the month, they might split and be ruined for next year. Remember to leave your cabbages in the ground until you get at least one or two light frosts, so that they have a little extra sweetness.

**November.** A time for reflection: What worked in the garden and what didn't? Label those dried seeds and set them aside. If the ground is still workable, add compost to the in-ground garden beds. Empty the hose and clean up your garden tools. If you are up for the challenge, get out the cold frames and try winter gardening (but that's a whole other book!).

**December.** This is the month most gardeners get to take off. If you skipped winter gardening, then take a break, make your Christmas list and enjoy a few days with clean fingernails—because everything will start up again soon!

# PLANTING 101

Planting a garden sounds so easy, yet I get something wrong *every single* year. And if I can screw it up, so can you! The exciting part of growing vegetables is that there is almost always something to do (as you'll know from the Planting Primer on the previous page), whether it's spring, summer, fall or even early winter. But the biggest mistake a first-time grower makes is starting too early. Always double-check your planting dates (see page 44) before you start.

## What to Plant

Once you've considered the pluses and minuses of your space (see pages 8–17)—including assessing both the sunlight and soil—you can start to plan for what it is that you should plant. The planning part here is key, and the motto RIGHT PLANT, RIGHT PLACE is so important when planning your garden. When we put plants in a spot where they will naturally thrive, they are health-ier plants and require less from us. Unfortunately, design and function don't always go hand in hand, and we force plants into spots where we want them to be, rather than where *they* want to be. This is bad news, as bugs and pathogens more easily invade a stressed-out plant because it is unable to fight them off effectively. It's like when you are tired from long hours at work: You are more likely to catch the office cold because your immune system is not at 100 percent. As you read through the descriptions of various plants in the following chapter (see page 92 onwards), pay careful attention to the conditions I list as helping the plants thrive, and be honest about whether that matches the conditions you have. You'll thank me in the long run.

**Knowing the best spots in your yard or on your property is the secret to having the best gardens. Not all locations are created equal!**

# Who Knew?!

## GOOD NEIGHBORS =GOOD GROWTH

As you plan your garden, be prepared for what I call the "wedding-table seating chart" otherwise known as my Good Growth Chart (page 59). If you have ever had to plan seating at a wedding reception, you know what I mean. Some guests get along better with others, and the same can be said of veggies. The following are a few stand out examples:

**Beans** are a problem child in the garden: There is a long list of vegetables they don't play nicely with or happily grow beside. Beware of having beans with any of the onion family. That means no leeks, no chives and no garlic near the beans! Beans and peppers are also not a good mix. I'm planting my beans near my corn, hoping that the corn will be strong enough to handle any stray runners.

**Tomatoes** are definitely considered the jewel of any vegetable plot because of their beauty and their flavor diversity. That said, I have quickly learned that they are also the princesses, with a lot of demands and specific needs. Several vegetables inhibit the growth of tomatoes, including all the brassicas (broccoli, cabbage, cauliflower and Brussels sprouts, for example). Corn, fennel and potatoes are also no-no's near your tomatoes. Instead, plant tomatoes with all the vegetables that your beans don't like—onions and peppers, for instance, will make tomatoes shine.

**Sage and thyme, or mint and oregano:** Plan to plant lots of these perennial herbs. They are the popular kids, getting along with almost every other veggie at school. Just be careful how you plant them, as they can take over your space.

| Vegetable | Plant with . . . | Avoid at all costs . . . |
|---|---|---|
| Asparagus | lettuce, spinach, tomatoes, strawberries | garlic, onions, potatoes |
| Beans | beets, cabbage, carrots, cauliflower, corn, parsnips | alliums (chives, garlic, leeks, onions, etc.); all peppers |
| Beets | asparagus, broccoli, cauliflower, lettuce, onions | climbing beans |
| Broccoli, Cabbages and Brussels Sprouts | beets, celery, onions, potatoes | tomatoes |
| Carrots | lettuce, onions, tomatoes | dill |
| Cauliflower | beans, beets, celery | broccoli, cabbage, strawberries, tomatoes |
| Celery | bush beans, cauliflower, spinach, tomatoes | corn |
| Corn | beans, cucumbers, potatoes | celery, tomatoes |
| Cucumbers | broccoli, cabbage, corn, lettuce, peas | potatoes |
| Eggplant | beans, lettuce, peas, potatoes | garlic, onions, peppers, sunflowers |
| Kale | cabbage, potatoes | tomatoes |
| Lettuce | everything . . . | . . . except broccoli! |
| Onions and Garlic | broccoli, cabbage, carrots, peppers (all), tomatoes | beans, peas |
| Peas | carrots, cucumbers, lettuce, potatoes | onions |
| Peppers (all) | (*love*) basil, onions, tomatoes | beans, eggplants |
| Potatoes | beans, cabbage, corn, eggplant, kale, lettuce, peas | cucumbers, tomatoes |
| Tomatoes | basil, chives, onions | cabbage, corn, fennel, potatoes |

**Consider incorporating plant diversity into your space. Lots of just one type of plant is more likely to attract insects that feed on that plant. By mixing plants all around your garden, you can create pairings that will fool many hungry predators. I like to add chives around lettuce: The smell of the chives keeps the bunnies away.**

## Companion Planting

*Companion planting* is about creating happy plants because happy plants grow more veggies. If you know that two or more plants grow well together, then plant them beside each other for a harmonious garden. So many plants have garden "frenemies" that hinder their growth. For this reason, check the Good Growth Chart (see page 59) for help in planning out your space—you need to know ahead of time what plays well with what. Companion planting is also an important consideration when planning your garden for the following year. Some plants are so picky when it comes to their mates that they don't even want to be planted in the same spot their nemesis was the year before. So with that in mind, make sure to track what went where each gardening season. If you plant peppers in a spot that had beans the year before, your peppers will not be happy, even a year later. Two-year gaps between plant frenemies is about right.

While still in the planning stages of planting, to plan the space most effectively I like to make seed (or garden) maps—yep, I'm a little type A that way! These maps help me lay out the garden beds according to companion planting and to make sure I have a spot for everyone. I also save my maps so that I can remember what grew well from year to year.

## Where to Plant: Shape and Spacing

**Always plant in rows, rather than circles.** Unless you are planting in a flowerpot, *straight lines* are really important. Since weed babies typically grow faster than veggie babies, you need to know where you planted your veggies so that you can confidently and safely

remove the weed competition if it starts to sprout. A straight line of little shoots is easier to identify. It is also easier to work around when weeding with a hoe or other tool.

**Plant your rows at least 8 inches apart** from each other, even if the veggies are going to stay small. Having enough space to run a tool between the rows will save you so much labor. Hand weeding is relaxing the first time you do it, but by the tenth time, you are going to be so over cleaning dirt out from under your nails. Make sure to give yourself the space to use a tool if you choose to.

**Follow the spacing instructions for each plant carefully.** If the seed pack says to sow the seeds 2 inches apart, do it. This seems totally obvious, but this is the one thing I screw up all the time. Lettuce and carrot seeds kill me because they are *so-o-o-o* tiny. I always plant them too close and then have to sacrifice some baby plants because they start to get crowded in the beds.

**Be sure to mark your seed rows.** Row markers are incredibly important (see my DIY on page 64). You need to know what you planted and where you planted it so you know where to water—especially if you are planting seeds in the soil versus seedlings that you started inside. This is critical because you will otherwise forget where the rows are until the plants start to grow. Even if you are like me and do a seed map ahead of time, having a physical reminder of what is in each row is crucial to understanding plant care, harvest times and even seed saving.

**Consider investing in a seeder** if you are planting a huge garden. Seeders are designed to dig the *furrow* (the row the seeds go into), plant the seed and then fill in the row with soil afterward. The good ones allow you to change the spacing so that seeds come out at exactly the right distance from each other. This is a major time saver. I bought one to help deal with the little seeds, like lettuces and carrots, because it is so hard to get the right spacing when you have big hands like mine!

# Row Markers

Row markers can be as simple as a painted rock or a Popsicle stick with the name of the veggie written on it. Here are a few suggestions:

**Write your labels using a waterproof marker.**
The markers will get wet, and it totally sucks when you have a blank row marker after the rain washes off the ink.

**Rewrite if necessary.** Sun will fade your writing. Be prepared to rewrite your labels if they start to fade.

**Use bright colors.** I swear that garden fairies move my markers, and I can then never find them when I need to. Bright, unnatural colors are more spot-able among the green leaves.

**Put the marker in the same spot on each row.**
It just makes life easier.

**Don't use seed packs.** My grandma used to put the seed packs on a stick and stick those in the dirt . . . *don't* do this! I'm not sure if the seed companies got cheap, but most of today's seed packs fade and wash out really fast, and then you won't know what you planted.

**Never use a seed marker with a sharp or pointy tip.** Lots of gardeners have poked themselves in the eye when weeding because they are focused on the ground and not what's in the periphery: pointy sticks.

## Seedlings

The directions on a seed pack will tell you all you need to know about the specifics of the seeds. This isn't always the case with seedlings. If you're planting seedlings, you'll want to make a hole in the dirt that is the same depth as the soil in the seedling pot. It is important to plant your babies at a depth they are already used to. Too deep or too shallow will affect the health of your plants as they struggle to adapt to the new surroundings.

# Good Gardeners Never Blame Their Tools

Your tools are totally your choice. Seriously, work with the tools that feel right to you and use them in the way that you want. The one thing you have to do is keep them clean and sharp. These are the tools I always have on hand:

**Hoe.** For weeding and trenching.

**Shovel.** For digging. A shovel that has a good sharp edge is better at digging and better for the plants. When you're dividing clumps or transplanting herbs, a sharp blade will cut through roots, so that you are not hacking at the poor plants—as you might be with a dull blade.

**Rake.** For making sure everything is level and pretty.

**Cutter.** Of some kind—scissors, knife or pruning shears—for, well, cutting. These are handy for harvesting vegetables, cutting back unruly plants and pruning.

**A hose and some sort of watering device.** You are going to spend all summer watering your plants, so invest in a good hose (one that doesn't easily get tangled or kink). You will also want a good nozzle for your hose. Unfortunately, the water pressure from most of our homes is too strong for small plants. Having a nozzle or a watering can will allow you to control the flow without damaging the tender shoots.

**Gloves.** I don't use gloves for gardening EXCEPT when I have to deal with things that are a) prickly or b) super gross and squishy. Lots of vegetables have spiny thorns designed to protect the plant. And gardening involves a fair amount of removing rotten or squishy things hiding under leaves, like slugs or old zucchinis. Choose gloves that fit well, are tough enough to protect your hands and are easy to wash.

**A rain gauge.** This is basically a beaker that has an open top and measurements on the side. As the rain falls, the beaker naturally collects the rainwater through the top and shows you how much your plants got. You can place your gauge beside plants that you are watering with a sprinkler to know when you have reached their desired weekly amount. I empty my rain gauge every Sunday so I know how much rain has fallen that week and how much more water I need to give my plants.

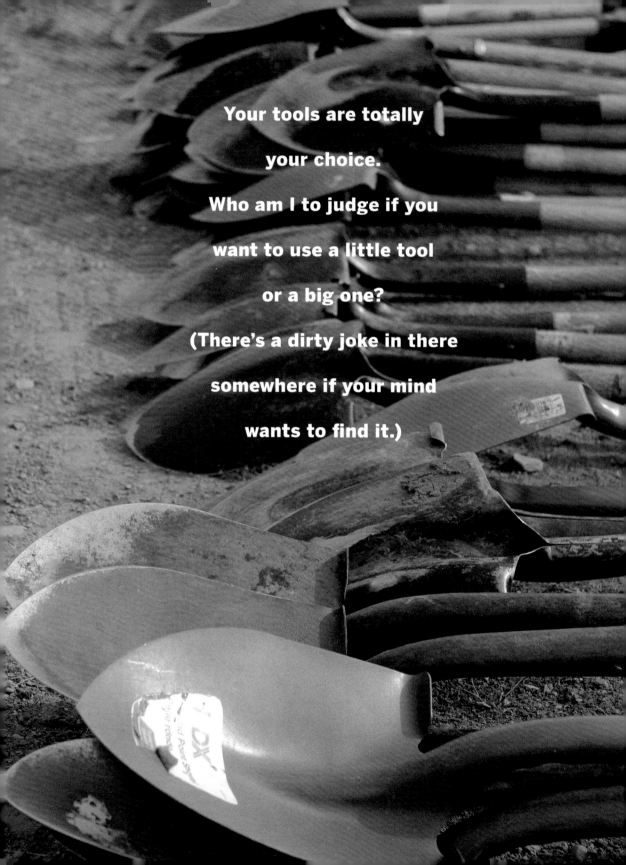

Your tools are totally

your choice.

Who am I to judge if you

want to use a little tool

or a big one?

(There's a dirty joke in there

somewhere if your mind

wants to find it.)

# Cleaning Your Tools

Cleaning your tools is important for stopping the spread of garden diseases. Yeah, there really are diseases in the garden—thankfully, they are mostly plant diseases. I am a huge advocate of cleaning my shovels, pruning shears, hoes and rakes at least once every week during gardening season. Here is how to do it:

1. Spray the tools with a high-pressure hose to remove clumps of dirt and mud.

2. Fill a spray bottle with equal parts rubbing alcohol and water.

3. Fill a large bucket with any type of plain sand (store-bought or gathered from the beach) and a large quantity of linseed oil. I like to use 5 parts sand to 1 part oil.

4. Douse your tools once a week with the spray bottle to disinfect them. Then plunge the metal parts of the tools into the bucket to coat them with the sand-oil mixture. This prevents the metal from rusting and readies the tools for the next time you use them.

# Multitasking Tool

Turn your shovel or rake into a measuring tool! This is such a simple idea I'm not sure why companies aren't selling such tools. I do it to every single gardening tool in my shed so that I always have a way to measure without having to get a measuring tape:

1. Using a permanent marker, mark 1-inch intervals on the handles of the gardening tools you use most often.

2. When planting, lay the handle alongside the row and, voilà, your seed spacing measurements are all right there.

# FEEDING YOUR GARDEN

## Water

When it comes to having a wicked garden full of lush veggies, water is right up there with the most important things you need. The trouble is that experts have differing opinions on how much water is the right amount. And since no two gardens have the same growing conditions, how can someone tell you what will work for you?

So how do you judge how much *your* garden needs? As a rule, vegetable plants need water at least 3 times per week, whether from rain or from you and your hose. Here are three ways to tell if they need more than that:

- Test the soil at least 1 inch below the surface. To do this, stick your finger into the soil to see if it feels moist. If it is dry down there, it's time to water.
- If the leaves of the plant look limp and droopy, it's time to water.
- If the ground or soil at the top of the pot is cracked, it's time to water.

Can you water too much? The short answer is yes. Studies show that more water usually makes for bigger vegetables, as in "The more you water, the more they grow." But this isn't always a good thing because water dilutes the natural sugars in several vegetables, including beets and many tomatoes. As a result, they have little to no flavor. Excess water can also cause some vegetables, including carrots and tomatoes, to split open. So it is possible to water too much. Your plant will tell you it has had too much through stunted growth or yellow, drooping lower leaves.

# Who Knew?!

## HOW MUCH WATER DO YOU NEED?

Here is what we do know: In the perfect growing situation, the average garden needs a minimum of 2 inches of water per week. But here are some caveats:

**If you have sandy soil.** You will need *more* water because the grains of sand don't hold moisture for the plants to use throughout the day.

**If you have clay soil.** You will need *less* water because the clay doesn't provide great drainage and therefore the soil holds more moisture.

**If you are growing in clay pots.** You need *more* water because the clay pots absorb the water from the soil and dry out the potting or mixed soil faster. We used to think the opposite was true . . . but now you know!

**If you are growing in the shade.** You need *less* water than if you are growing in full sun. A desert is always dry because the sun evaporates the available water. More light also means the plant has the ability to produce more energy through photosynthesis . . . and needs more water to do it!

# Watering Myths

**Myth 1** Never water your plants when it's sunny outside, because the water droplets work like a magnifying glass, intensifying the sunlight and leading to scorched leaves.

**Truth** Your plants are naturally designed to do just fine with wet leaves in full sun. Water them when they need it.

**Myth 2** Always water your plants from below the leaves of the plant.

**Truth** Experts have always said to water plants from below to prevent mildew and fungal growth, but recent studies show that sometimes plants need a little moisture on the leaves to help remove dust and buildup. The important thing is to make sure you soak the leaves *and* the soil to ensure that the water is getting to the roots.

## Self-Watering Devices

If you plant in containers, you need to pay particular attention to the moisture levels of the soil. Your plants are in their own mini ecosystems, unable to access water or nutrients from anywhere other than their planter, and they rely on you for pretty much everything. Whenever I plant in a pot, I always include some sort of self-watering device. Kind of like a patient-controlled pain button in a hospital. This gives the plant the water it needs on-demand, as the system adds moisture to the soil as it naturally dries out.

### Glass Watering Globes

A *glass watering globe* or bulb is a round sphere with a long stem, and it's a personal favorite of mine because it looks so good in the pot. It's pretty easy to use: Just fill the ball with water through the hollow stem and stick the stem into the soil deep enough that it won't fall over.

There is one small trick to making this apparatus work: You need to make sure that some of the soil gets jammed up in the stem, kind of like a dirt plug. You can double-check that this happened by pushing it into the pot and then pulling it back out to see if there is soil in the stem. This trick is also the only downside to the system, because you need to get the damn soil out again when you have to refill the watering globe. I use a chopstick to poke the soil into the body of the globe, and then fill the globe with lots of water and swish it around until the soil washes out.

As the soil in the pot dries out, the water in the bulb is slowly released through the dirt plug. It's hard to say exactly how long a globe will last between refills—it depends on the size of the globe and how thirsty your plant is. That said, it's super easy to tell when the water has run out, because you can just look at the bulb to see if there's water left inside. If you're planning to use glass watering globes to water while you're on vacation, do a test before you leave to see how long they last.

### Clay Watering Systems

Another option is a *clay watering system*, which is an unglazed clay or terra cotta reservoir buried in the soil right by the roots of the plants. One open end of the pot (or sometimes, an attached water bottle) sticks out above the surface, so you can add more water without removing the whole thing. The clay is porous, so the water in the container seeps into the soil and waters the plant.

The downside of this method is that the reservoir needs to be planted right beside the plants in among their roots. As the plants grow, the roots naturally head toward the water

source, so you can get a dense bunch of roots all clustered around (and sometimes inside) the clay reservoir.

### Tech Watering Systems

*Tech watering systems* are watering devices that use timers and pumps to water your plants. They are pretty awesome when they work. The problem with these systems is that it's easy to accidentally rely on them a little too much. I got a shock when my system's battery died while I was away and all my plants died because no one checked on them. If you decide to go the tech route, make sure to check the power source for your system before you head out of town!

**DIY**

# Watering System

When it comes to DIY tricks for watering your plants, there are thousands of suggestions out there. They almost all have one thing in common, though: They look like hell! (IMHO)

You can easily make your own very effective—and not unattractive—watering system by recycling any bottle with a narrow neck. Wine bottles are my favorite to use because I have a lot available.

**If you have a screw-top version:**

1. Remove the label from the bottle (because no one needs to know the cheap stuff that you've been having with pizza on Fridays nights, and Saturdays . . .).

2. Poke a small hole into the cap.

3. Wash and then fill the bottle with clean water.

4. Replace the cap.

5. Stick the bottle upside down in the planter.

**For a corked bottle:**

1. Remove the label.

2. Push the cork $2/3$ of the way back into the bottle.

3. Use a small drill bit or a nail to widen the hole made by the corkscrew, so that it goes right through the cork.

4. Remove the cork.

5. Wash and then fill the bottle with clean water.

6. Replace the cork (the deeper you insert it into the bottle, the slower the water will come out).

7. Stick the bottle upside down in the planter.

# Food

Feeding your garden means adding nutrients to the soil that the plants need for optimum growth (see page 14). Every year that you have a garden in the same space, the plants in that space use up more and more of the nutrients naturally found in the soil there, which means fewer and fewer nutrients will be there the next year and the years after that—leaving your soil in much need of a vitamin and mineral top-up!

One of the most important aspects of *organic gardening* (something I'm an advocate for) is feeding the *soil* using natural materials instead of fertilizing the *plant* with chemical compounds or growth enhancements. If you focus on the soil and what the plant is using to feed itself through its roots, you can achieve increased growth without the use of fertilizers. Feeding the soil means adding healthy additives to it to promote the right kind of natural organisms and plant life. This is where *composting* comes in. By adding decomposing plants (also called *organic matter*), we can emulate the way in which plants and trees get nutrients in the wild—living off rotting leaves, branches and fallen trees. Another way to feed your soil is with *manure*, and I'll go over the best poo for you on page 80. You can also consider planting *cover crops* to give off healthy nutrients to the plants that will follow them (more about this on page 81).

## Compost

Composting is nature's way of providing nutrients to plants. Through the process of decomposition, organic matter is transformed into nutrient-rich soil, perfect to mix with the existing soil. Compost can be built solely out of leaves and grass clippings. Or it can be mixed with many other "ingredients," like paper, wood, manure, and fruit and vegetable scraps, as well as any other kitchen scraps (as long as they are not protein based). It's a great way to keeps things out of the landfill! It takes 6 months to a year to produce soil through composting, so be patient. To speed up the process, regularly mix the compost, to allow air and rain into the pile. You can add water periodically when it's dry outside, to help the composting process along. Turning the hose on for 10 minutes will encourage natural fibers to break down

**One of the most important aspects of *organic gardening* (something I'm an advocate for) is feeding the *soil* using natural materials instead of fertilizing the *plant* with chemical compounds or growth enhancements.**

faster than when they are dry. If your compost is smelly, back off on the watering; the compost has had enough. Any of the following items always work well in a compost mix:

**Ashes.** Whether from your fireplace, fire pit or campfire, ashes are a fantastic source of lime and potassium, among other minerals. Just make sure that they are completely cold before adding to the heap, so that you don't start a forest fire.

**Coffee grounds.** These add acidity to the compost, which is a good thing for many types of crops, especially blueberries. Dumping coffee grounds into the composter will help nature create the perfect blend of soil. I add the grounds from my coffeepot twice a week. If you are a heavy espresso drinker and have a lot of espresso grounds, only add them once a week because they tend to be stronger.

**Eggshells.** As a natural source of calcium, eggshells are a perfect addition to your compost mix and, in turn, an easy and natural way to add calcium to your garden beds. By increasing the calcium levels in the ground, you can avoid some of the crappy parts of vegetable growing, like the dreaded blossom-end rot on tomatoes and cucumbers. Don't be worried if the shells haven't completely broken down by the time you spread the soil around your plants.

**Hair.** Your hair and your pet's hair are super sources of nitrogen, which gets released into the compost pile and eventually makes its way to the plants. (This also is true of toenail clippings. I know it sounds a little gross—but trust me on this one.)

# Big, nasty, wiggling, wet worms sold at fishing-supply stores are amazing for your compost pile!

**Laundry lint.** All that lint that comes out of your clothes dryer is an excellent source of nutrients for the compost heap. When adding it, spread it out so that it breaks down faster.

**Manure.** See page 80 for why manure is good for your soil, and therefore a good add to the compost pile. (Just make sure to follow all the steps to properly handle it!)

**Worms.** Big, nasty, wiggling, wet worms sold at fishing-supply stores are amazing for your compost pile! Worms eat the waste and poop out fertilizer gold! In fact, you can actually buy worm poo to spread around your plants for the nutrient benefits. Worms do most of their best work in early spring and late fall, when the compost pile typically contains relatively high levels of natural moisture. If you want to add worms in summertime, just make sure to water the pile well first.

## Creating a Composter

Building a composter is not rocket science—after all, you're just making a spot for crap to rot! Even a pile of clippings and weeds will eventually turn into a compost heap. There are many options for composters, but all of them fall into three categories:

**The Heap.** Just keep piling everything into one messy heap, and every now and then flip the pile with a shovel or pitchfork. This method is as cheap and easy as it gets. However, animals love compost. If you are in an urban area and don't have space to keep your pile out of sight, definitely skip this method. You'll have eggshells and crap spread everywhere. Gotta love those raccoons!

**Wood or Mesh Cage.** Build a wood or mesh cage to hold everything inside as it breaks down. If critters are an issue, you can add a lid so they don't get into it. To be able to access the good stuff once it's broken down (usually after a few years with this method), you'll want to add a door at the bottom. I screwed a board on the bottom that I can easily remove by taking out the six screws holding it in place. Now I can access the nutrient-rich soil whenever I need it. This is a super straightforward and low-cost option, but it does have a few challenges. For one, you have to make sure the compost has good airflow and lots of water, as both are important to the composting process. Also, having everything enclosed like this makes it harder to stir the pile as it gets packed down and binds together, so the composting process takes longer than the other methods listed here.

**Premade.** Super easy to use, with assembly and usage instructions, these ready-to-go systems are low effort and pretty good at minimizing smells, so they're especially good for both rooftops and backyards. But I find that they fill up really fast. Or maybe I just have too much waste to put in them! Most premade composters are best for batch composting and need to be emptied before you start the composting process over. They are, however, fast at producing compost from your kitchen waste.

**In northern climates that have one growing season per year, add just 1 to 3 inches of compost to your garden beds once a year, in the fall.**

### How Much Do I Use?

In northern climates that have one growing season per year, add just 1 to 3 inches of compost to your garden beds once a year, in the fall. (If you have crappy soil or soil that is really light in color (sand or clay), add more compost, up to 6 inches.) Place the compost right on top of the soil, leave it there for the winter and then work it into the garden just before you plant in the spring.

In southern areas, which might have multiple growing seasons, add your compost (max of 6 inches) at the end of each growing season and work it well into the soil before you plant the next crop.

### Manure

Manure, like compost, is an excellent source of nutrients that will help your plants grow. As with compost (see page 75), adding manure to your soil helps replace what might be missing. Before you run out to your local farm to collect cow poop though, there are a few things you need to know.

The first is that raw manure releases large amounts of nitrogen, which can burn plants, so it must be composted for at least a year before being used in the garden. Bagged manure from the garden center is often sterilized before being packaged. This is an important step, as manure is full of E. coli and other pathogens. If you are using raw manure, composting it before using will kill the bad stuff. This sterilization also helps kill the weed seeds that are naturally passed through the animal and would otherwise end up in your garden.

If you are unsure how long raw manure has been in the compost pile, you can still use it—just make sure not to spread it around your vegetables within 4 months of harvesting them.

### The Best Poo?

Not all poo is created equal. These are some of the most popular manure options for your veggies:

**Alpaca.** Alpacas are ruminants (cud chewers) with three stomachs. Their process of digestion reduces the consumed organic matter and allows the manure to go into your garden with less composting. Alpaca manure is also odor-free, which is a plus for the gardener!

**Chicken.** This is definitely the best for your leafy greens, as it contains high amounts of nitrogen. The high nitrogen levels also mean that you need to be extra diligent in ensuring that the chicken manure is well composted, or it will do damage to your tender plants for sure.

**Cow.** Cows have multiple stomachs, which means they are pretty good at digesting their food and breaking down the organic matter, including many (but not all) of the weed seeds they consume. Cow manure is considered lower in nutritional value for your plants than store-bought fertilizers, but it should still be considered an excellent all-purpose amendment for your existing soil.

**Horse.** A good all-purpose soil conditioner but one relatively low in nutrients. The big issue with horse manure is that because of horses' digestive systems, they process only about a quarter of the weed seeds they consume. The rest go straight into your garden via their manure and start to grow. The other big red flag is that we medicate horses for a lot of things, and the excess medicines that the horse's bodies get rid of end up in their poop.

**Sheep.** This is often drier than other manures, making it easier to work with. But, like cow and horse manure, sheep poo can badly burn tender plants. It is also often full of weed seeds—sheep are notorious for eating almost everything in the pasture.

## Cover Crops

Planting cover crops is a great way to replace nutrients in the soil over large areas and a technique used by farmers to grow their own fertilizers right in the field that needs it. Cover crops work very well for gardens in need of a little pick-me-up. This is how it works: A cover crop—annual rye grass, for instance—is planted in late summer or early fall, at the end of the vegetable-growing season, and left to grow until spring when they are ploughed into the ground. Peas, grasses and mustards, among other crops, all increase the organic matter in a beneficial way because they replace nitrogen and add extra nutrients as they naturally break down into the soil. It's sort of like mass composting.

> **Planting cover crops is a great way to replace nutrients in the soil over large areas and a technique used by farmers to grow their own fertilizers right in the field that needs it.**

# A LITTLE
# MORE LOVE
# & CARE

## Weeds

A weed is something that has no purpose. That's it! Really, a weed is anything that you don't want in your garden. Some flowers are considered weeds by some gardeners but treasures by others. Weeds may not do direct damage to the plants you are trying to grow, but they may suck up the nutrients in the soil that could be put to better use for your veggies. Or they may just be plain ugly. Is it a weed? Does it got to go? Ultimately, it's up to you to decide the value of the plants you choose to care for. New gardeners always ask me how to tell a weed from a plant. Follow the simple flow chart (page 86–87) to help you answer this question.

### Weed-Removal Techniques

Once you know which are weeds, the best way to get rid of them is to rip those babies out by the roots. Ripping out weeds is a pain in the ass and probably one of the worst jobs you'll have to do in the garden. There are all kinds of tools out there to help you, but ultimately, you need to get down to the weed's roots and get them all out of the ground so that they won't grow again. Sometimes even that's not enough—some weeds have an awesome ability to spread seeds everywhere, so ripping the weeds out doesn't really help stop the seeds that have already hit the ground. Which is why big business makes a lot of money from chemical weed killers. Using chemical weed killers is for sure the easy way to get rid of weeds. Unfortunately, some of them are pretty harmful to the environment—and to you and your family if they are absorbed into the food. The great news is there are natural alternatives.

Pulling weeds after a rain shower is *always* easier than pulling them out before. When the soil is damp, the roots of the plant release much easier. When it's dry, the little buggers can cling to the ground better.

## Vinegar Spray

As an alternative to chemical weed killer, I use cleaning-strength or double-strength white vinegar that has an acid content stronger than 6%. I put this in a spray bottle and go at the weeds among the patio stones and on the driveway. The vinegar will kill the part of the plant it comes in contact with and often wipe out the roots below as well. You may have to repeat the process a few times to ensure you have all of the plant but be very careful using this stuff around your veggies, as it can wipe out entire sections of your garden if you're not careful. Remember, you can't control what is happening below the surface, and sprays and liquids can easily spread, killing beneficial plants, insects and microorganisms.

## Elimination Method

If you're using neither chemicals nor vinegar around your green babies, you'll need to find a way to eliminate one of the three things that weeds need to grow: water, soil and sunlight:

**Water.** This is the toughest of the three to block. Rain won't stop falling on command, and some weeds need way less water than your plants do, so you'd really need a drought to get results. Short answer: forget trying to waterproof your garden.

**Mulch over the soil.** Some weeds can grow in pretty much anything—just the dust on the side of the patio, or even just the gunge that collects between the boards of your deck. But most weeds need actual soil to grow in, so putting down a layer of mulch on top of the soil is a good way to prevent new weeds from growing. Although mulch will help prevent weed seeds from getting down to the soil below, it won't help the ones that are already in the ground (you'll still have to deal with those once they grow up through the layer of mulch).

**Sunlight.** When the other two options fail, as they inevitably will, focus on stopping the weeds from getting sunlight. You can eliminate weeds in this way by using one of a few methods:

- 🍎 **Carpet.** Okay, no joke: My grandma used to put old carpet down in between rows to stop the weeds from growing, and it totally worked. It looked like hell, but it worked!
- 🍎 **Landscape fabric.** If you can't get past the 1950s throwback carpet idea, use geotextile (landscape fabric) instead. It works the same way and looks a hell of a lot better. In fact, throw mulch on top of the fabric and you have a winner!

**Newspaper.** You're too cheap to buy carpet or landscape fabric? Then use newspaper with mulch spread on top. Seven layers of newspaper will kill everything underneath it and then naturally break down so that you don't have to ever see or deal with it again. Sounds like the perfect ex!

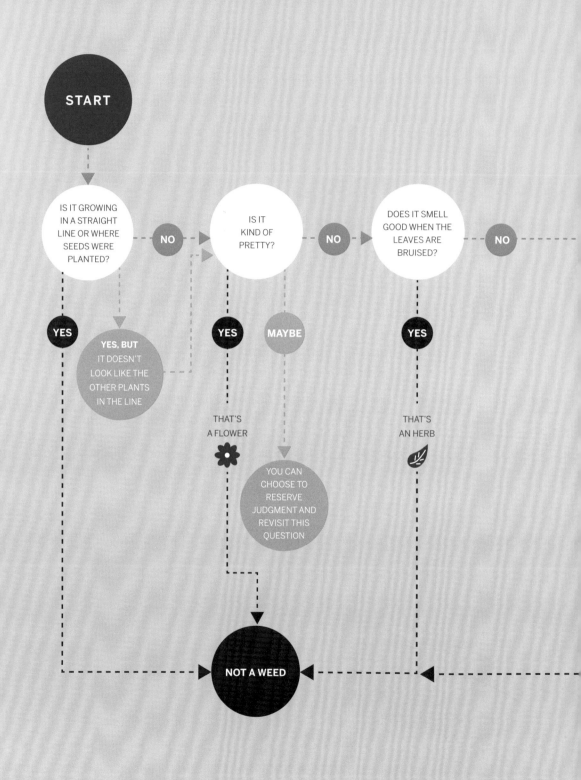

START

IS IT GROWING IN A STRAIGHT LINE OR WHERE SEEDS WERE PLANTED?

NO

IS IT KIND OF PRETTY?

NO

DOES IT SMELL GOOD WHEN THE LEAVES ARE BRUISED?

NO

YES

YES, BUT IT DOESN'T LOOK LIKE THE OTHER PLANTS IN THE LINE

YES

MAYBE

YES

THAT'S A FLOWER

YOU CAN CHOOSE TO RESERVE JUDGMENT AND REVISIT THIS QUESTION

THAT'S AN HERB

NOT A WEED

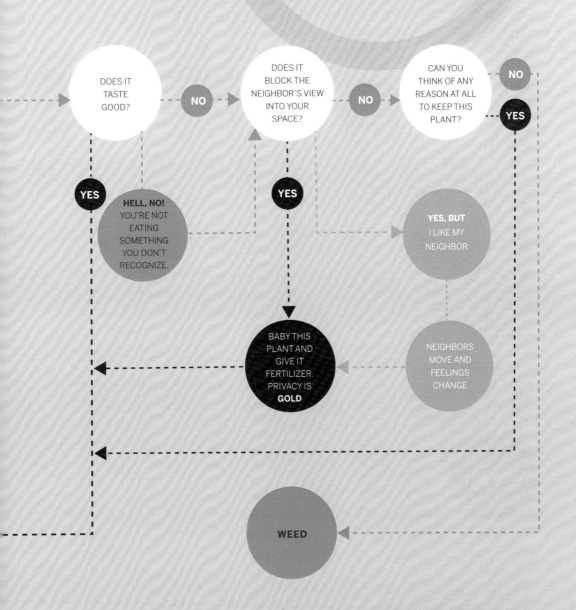

# WEED FLOWCHART

DOES IT TASTE GOOD?

NO

DOES IT BLOCK THE NEIGHBOR'S VIEW INTO YOUR SPACE?

NO

CAN YOU THINK OF ANY REASON AT ALL TO KEEP THIS PLANT?

NO

YES

YES

**HELL, NO!** YOU'RE NOT EATING SOMETHING YOU DON'T RECOGNIZE.

YES

**YES, BUT** I LIKE MY NEIGHBOR

BABY THIS PLANT AND GIVE IT FERTILIZER. PRIVACY IS **GOLD**

NEIGHBORS MOVE AND FEELINGS CHANGE

**WEED**

# Protecting from Pests

Pests are bad news for plants. Pests eat your vegetables before you can. Keeping your plants growing while avoiding pests is the biggest challenge facing every gardener. And pests come in so many shapes and sizes: bugs, birds, slugs, bunnies, dogs, cats, small children, neighbors ... they are all pests when it comes to your food and having to protect it.

There are lots of ways to protect your plants using natural methods instead of synthetic products. Just remember that these methods are not foolproof. Your plants are going to get a certain level of insect damage, and that is totally okay. So let's look at some of the best simple concoctions that help protect plants from certain pests.

**Bugs.** Blasting your plants with a high-pressure water hose is a great way to remove caterpillars and slugs (and strangely satisfying at the same time). You can also purchase insecticidal soaps or horticultural oils from any garden center or make your own (see DIY on this page). Insecticidal soap kills soft-body insects like aphids when they come in contact with it. Horticultural oil is a little more aggressive than insecticidal soap and should be used for severe infestations. You could also try garlic water as a natural and environmentally friendly bug repellent (see my DIY on page 90). When all else fails, premade mesh tunnels placed over your plants will effectively stop flying insects from invading them.

## Insecticidal Soap

To make your own insecticidal soap, mix 5 tablespoons of plain dish soap with 1 gallon of clean water. Make sure to avoid concentrated or antibacterial dish soap, as these can harm your plants.

**Cats.** Put whole cinnamon sticks around the edges of your garden beds. Whenever it rains or you water the garden, the fragrant scent of cinnamon will waft through your space and encourage those roaming felines to find another litter box. Although we love the fragrant scent, cats hate it.

**Dogs.** Substitute orange and lemon peels for the garlic (see Garlic Water, page 90), to make a citrus spray that the neighborhood dogs won't be able to stand. Spray your citrus mix anywhere that any dogs are marking their territory, and they will move on.

## Garlic Water

Throw 12 cloves of unpeeled garlic into a large clear pail or jug. Fill with 1 gallon of clean water. Leave the container outside in the sun (clear containers work best as the sun will help break down the garlic cloves), covered, for a few days to make a strong garlic tea. Strain out the cloves and the skins and then pour the smelly water into a spray bottle. Spray the leaves, flowers and stems of the plant after each rain to safely coat them with an unappetizing shield against beetles, aphids and slugs.

**Rabbits and squirrels.** Avoid using cayenne pepper to deter rabbits and squirrels. This method has been proven effective, though getting the amount right is harder than you may think. Too much and you can cause the wildlife a lot of pain, burning their nostrils and eyes. Instead of chancing that, spread a little used cat litter around the perimeter of your garden beds. Rabbits and squirrels are terrified of cats and will avoid any spots that felines visit.

**Raccoons.** If you have raccoons and you don't have a large dog to keep them out of your space, it might be time to move. Kidding! (Sort of.) Raccoons are tough to keep out of any space once they have established themselves. Your vegetable garden is a salad bar waiting to happen for these animals that eat pretty much anything. The only successful deterrent that I know of for raccoons is human urine, especially male urine. Think of it like marking your territory, and pee on the planter! Human urine loses most of its smell outdoors after just a few days so you may have to repeat if the raccoons come back.

## Keep It Clean

Yep, having plants can be messy. Water and soil are the two big contributors to this. Water leaks and soil stains. And combine the two and you have mud. I point out this aspect of gardening because even though it may seem totally obvious, many first-time gardeners try to find ways around the inevitable mess, with limited success. In a backyard, it's easy to deal with water, soil and mud—you sweep it into the yard or garden bed. But in a contained area like a patio, it's not so easy.

Almost all plants do best when they can be wet and then dry and then wet again. So you want to allow the water to drain from the pots and planters—and as it mixes with the soil, you get a muddy mess at the bottom of the planters. There are things that will help keep down the mess though, that really do provide benefits.

**Diapers—clean ones, please!** The white powder in a disposable diaper liner—hydrogel— is the same stuff florists add to the water in a vase, to keep cut flowers hydrated. The beauty of using this product in your planter is that each average diaper can hold up to 9 cups of water, and the plants will absorb moisture from this as they need. To use diapers, remove the liners by tearing open the diapers (recycle the rest). Then line your containers with the diaper liners. Ideally, you want liners that are either white or clear; the plants will absorb the dye otherwise, and who wants to eat diaper dye?

**Landscape fabric.** Also called geotextile, this is a black woven fabric used to keep the soil in the pot, even when the water comes out. Available at almost any garden center or big-box store, landscape fabric can be easily cut to fit whatever container you are gardening with. Line the bottom and sides of the pot and partially up the sides—just don't bring the fabric too close to the top or you will see it there as the soil contracts with time.

**Self-watering containers.** These purchasable planters are a great option for homeowners who are away a lot. The system is pretty simple: Because of their design, the planters keep water in a reservoir below the roots, so that the roots do not sit directly in water but can access it as needed. The reservoir holds a lot of water, which means you don't have to fill it often. There is also a filter or barrier that keeps the soil from mixing with the water— helpful in reducing mess. These are great for any type of garden but work especially well for rooftop and balcony gardens, where space saving is important, or where the garden is underneath a balcony and doesn't get a lot of rain.

**Styrofoam peanuts.** This packing material is often used as lightweight filler at the bottom of a garden container, so that the container doesn't get too heavy and can be easily moved; it also cuts down on the cost of expensive soil. A lot of gardening purists resist the idea of using a man-made material because of concerns about the product leaching into the food. Several online reports, including those of the US-based National Toxicology Program, list it as a possible cancer-causing agent but go on to explain that the Styrofoam does not contaminate food and can be safely used around vegetables.

My grandma used to put rocks in the bottom of her pots. Her theory was that water would drain through the soil onto the rocks and away from the plant, but science has proven that soil will absorb, and keep absorbing, the water until it can't hold any more moisture. (So, basically, the rocks just add weight, which totally sucks if in a pot that you want to move regularly.)

# VEGETABLES: THE VEGGIES

In this section I'm going to look at a few of the best veggies to consider planting in your space, and give you the lowdown on what they need to survive. It may take you a couple of tries to grow the veggie garden of your dreams, but the results are worth it—and there's no shame in a *#gardenfail* or two along the way. Remember, your vegetables don't care if your garden is perfect. They're going to do their best to grow and thrive, no matter what you throw at them.

# Asparagus

PLANT IN EARLY SPRING.
HARVEST 3 YEARS LATER!

{ FULL SUN }

**Asparagus is one of my favorite** vegetables to eat, but you have to have some patience to grow it. It will take you about 3 years to harvest your first asparagus crop, and for some gardeners that's a long wait. The good news is that once it's established, an asparagus plant can last over 20 years, with very little effort or maintenance. *Score!* And because these little stems of goodness are getting more expensive to buy in the grocery store every year, growing your own will also save you lots of money: My family eats at least one bunch per week, which equals almost $300 a year!

## Sunlight

Asparagus does best in full sun but can be planted near deciduous trees (ones that lose their leaves in the winter) because the asparagus will be harvested before the leaves of the tree grow to create full shade.

## Dirt

Use nutrient-dense dirt with lots of compost. Asparagus plants like loose soil so they can spread and grow into a healthy clump.

## Space

Most asparagus is grown in the ground, but if you are a condo dweller, it's worth noting that asparagus can do well in an insulated planter. Just make sure that the pot is at least 28 inches deep and 36 inches wide so that the plants have enough space.

## Plant

The parts of the asparagus that most people eat are the tender shoots that grow out of the roots starting just below the surface. Plant these bare-root crowns in early spring and harvest the shoots in the third growing year. Dig a hole about a foot deep and add lots of compost and nutrient-rich soil to the planter or bed, because these plants thrive on the good stuff. Put some soil on top of the compost and place the roots in the hole so that the crown is 1 inch below the surface. Add more compost and lots of loose mulch. Plant your asparagus about 2 feet apart to allow lots of light and airflow.

Growing asparagus from seeds is an option, but the crowns are the faster way to go because when you plant them they are already at least a year or two old. They are often available at garden centers or online.

## Care

Keep your asparagus clump moist but not saturated. Asparagus plants do not like to be sitting in a puddle of water. The frequency of additional watering will depend on your local weather, such as amount of rainfall, sunlight and average daytime temperature.

For the first and second years, asparagus will send up tall fernlike shoots that often have red berries on them. You might want to stake them, but leave these shoots alone, as they will help grow bigger roots under the soil. You can then remove them once they start to yellow in late fall. Be prepared to have massive fronds—some breeds of asparagus like Jersey Giant can send up fronds that are 7 feet tall and can create a thick shade on any other vegetables growing near them. So keep this in mind when you're planning where to plant your asparagus, and with what.

Asparagus is a favorite food of several insects, including the asparagus beetle. Plant herbs that have a strong scent—such as basil, parsley and dill—around your asparagus crowns to fool the bugs.

## Harvest

In year 3 it's time to harvest! Harvest based on how you like to eat asparagus. If you prefer skinny spears, you may be harvesting every day starting in early spring as the spears grow out of the soil. For thicker spears, wait longer. Use a sharp knife or your pruners to cleanly cut off the spears at ground level but be careful not to cut into or damage the crown. These spears can be eaten right away, but if not, make sure the bottoms are submerged in water immediately and they are stored in the fridge.

## Prepare for Next Year

You can only harvest asparagus for about 6 weeks. After that you need to stop and let the plant recuperate. It does this by growing the fernlike shoots again and feeding itself for the rest of the summer. If you have red berries growing on your plant, consider harvesting these and drying them out in the sun to save for planting or sharing with your neighbor! Yellow stalks in the fall should be removed to allow for new growth in the spring.

**My very first gardening** experience was all about beans! We got to grow them in a Styrofoam cup in grade one. OOOOH! I remember the 2 leaves and the pretty cup but have absolutely no idea what happened with the plant from that point onward. Needless to say, beans are easy to grow! Stick them in warm(ish) soil and they start.

# Beans

PLANT DIRECTLY IN THE GARDEN
AFTER THE LAST FROST

{ FULL SUN }

## Varieties

There are 2 main ways that beans grow: on poles (climbers) and on bushes (not climbers). I kind of went bean-crazy my first few times and bought a lot, leaving no room for anything else . . . so use some restraint the first time you order. When it comes to choosing your beans, there are thousands of options available, but all of them can be broken down into the main types below.

**Snap beans.** The ones that your grandma would serve you steamed to eat with a protein. Look for varieties that are "string-less" and don't have the fibrous thread that runs down the backside of each bean. (I am also a sucker for the sugar-snap bean just because I like to say the name with a Southern accent.)

**Wax beans.** The yellow version of the green snap bean. These are also sometimes purple or red.

**Soy, lima, dry, butter.** All names of beans grown for what is inside the pod. These often take longer to grow because the plant first develops the protective pod and then the beans inside of it.

**Runner beans.** These are climbers and are not really known for eating; instead, they are usually grown for their flowers and are a staple in a cottage flower garden. These beans have a poisonous root, so if you have a dog that likes to dig and eat random things, beware!

**Yard-long beans.** SO-O-O-O-O cool for kids. These beans grow super long and are often in crazy colors or have great spots. These come in both pole and bush varieties.

### Sunlight

All beans grow best in full sun.

### Dirt

Well-drained soil—beans do not do as well in clay or heavy soil situations.

### Space

**Pole beans.** Some varieties can grow upward of 8 feet. The key to the success of this type of bean is that they need something to twine around, as pole beans can't climb up walls. They grow with shoots that twist around a trellis or a fence, propelling the plant higher and higher.

**Bush beans.** Bush beans are NOT climbers, so these are the ones that you want for patios and balconies. Bush beans max out at about 2–3 feet tall, making them very manageable for almost any garden.

### Plant

Plant your beans directly into the garden once the threat of frost has passed. They don't do so well with the cold, and because they have shallow roots, they don't transplant well. This applies to planting in-ground or in a container on your balcony. Just make sure the soil is warm to the touch. Leave it in a very sunny spot. Beans love the heat! As a rule, beans need to be planted ¼ inch deep into the ground and about 4–6 inches apart.

### Care

Beans require moderate water: 1–2 inches per week will be plenty to keep them happy. Don't fertilize your beans. They are one of a few vegetables that actually improve the soil where they live. Sort of like the home renovator in the garden.

Beans are susceptible to a variety of diseases. There are a couple of general rules if you think your bean plant is unhealthy. First, to prevent the spread of the disease, never do any gardening work like weeding or hoeing around the plant when it is wet from dew or rain. Second, if the plant is clearly ill (is covered with yellowed leaves, for example, or has rot forming on the stems), rip it out! You can't save it and you don't want it spreading to the others.

### Harvest

Beans are harvested at the stage that you want to eat them. Just remember, the longer you leave a bean on the plant, the tougher the skin becomes, and it will start to taste woody and chewy. Make sure to check your plants every few days, as they grow fast in the heat. Snap beans should be picked when they are young and tender. Harvesting beans that are grown inside a pod is tricky, because you want them to get as large as possible inside the pod, kind of like a pea. Make sure to keep checking these as the beans start to form.

### Prepare for Next Year

Saving beans for next year is pretty easy. Just leave several pods on the plant until they completely dry out and turn brown. The beans inside are perfect for planting next spring if you keep them in a dark and dry space.

# Beets

PLANT DIRECTLY IN THE GARDEN
IN EARLY SPRING OR LATE FALL

{ FULL SUN PREFERABLY,
BUT CAN HANDLE SOME SHADE }

**Beets are one of the easiest and** most amazing plants to have in your garden, whether you eat the tiny shoots as a microgreen, use the leaves the same way you would spinach or wait for the perfect little gems to grow under the soil. Versatile beets are a cook's best friend.

## Sunlight

Beets like full sun but can handle some shade, especially in the middle of the day when it is the warmest.

## Dirt

Beets love a loose soil that will allow them to grow big, healthy roots with minimal struggle.

## Space

Beets can be grown in-ground, in raised beds or even in some large pots. Just re-member that beets grow BELOW the ground, so they need space for their roots.

## Plant

Beets are best planted in early spring or in late fall because they get bitter in the heat. (I know too many people just like that!) If you live in a colder climate where the ground freezes each year, wait at least 2–3 weeks after the ground has thawed before you plant. In a container or on a balcony, beets can go in once the snow has melted. The other time to plant beets is about 6 weeks before frost. In my area, I like to plant a couple of rows at the end of August. I leave these plants in the ground until after the first frost of the year because the cold makes the roots sweeter. YUM!

Before planting, soak your beet seeds in a glass of water overnight to help speed up the germination process. The extra moisture gets the little guys growing even faster and more seeds will grow. Beets like to be planted about ½ inch in the ground and about 2 inches apart. This can be tricky, as the seeds are brutally small. Be patient planting them.

## Care

Consistent watering keeps your beets happy. You don't have to drench them; just give them a good splash every few days. Beets have very few needs, which is why

I kind of love them. If you want to eat the tops, keep an eye out for insect damage early and treat with insecticidal soap (see page 88).

## Harvest

If you are eating the tops of the plants, harvest away based on size. The general rule is the smaller the sweeter, but the bigger the more intense the flavor. I like to harvest mine when the leaves are about 2 inches long. If you want the roots, you can still trim a few of the leaves for eating, but make sure to keep some so that the plant is able to produce food to grow a healthy root.

You may also have to sacrifice a few beet babies so that the others will produce larger roots. Pick the healthiest plants (the ones with the most leaves) and remove all the other ones in between. Aim for about 2 inches between plants to allow for the best chance at growing big. I like to harvest my beets when they get to be the size of a medium egg.

## Prepare for Next Year

Beets will produce seeds that you can harvest; however, they only do this every second year. Plants that do this are called *biennials* and need to be protected over the winter as roots so that they can have a second summer to develop seeds. In colder climates, store your beets in a root cellar or in a cool, dark basement, then plant them again the following year. In areas with a mild winter, leave a few beets in the ground and bury them in a heavy blanket of mulch. When the time comes to harvest, cut off their tall stalks, remove the seeds and store in a paper bag.

# Brassicas

## (Broccoli, Cauliflower, Cabbages, Brussels Sprouts and Kale)

START INDOORS, 4-6 WEEKS
BEFORE MOVING OUTSIDE

{ SUNLIGHT VARIES
BETWEEN VARIETIES }

**Brassicas are a whole group of** plants in the mustard family. Often, they have stems or stalks as a common link. (Another common link . . . they all give me gas! TMI?)

## Varieties

**Broccoli and cauliflower** are two of the most common brassicas. Both clearly form on a stiff stalk and grow almost identically, with one exception: Sprouting broccoli is a unique group that sends up lots of little shoots instead of one big one. Considered a wonder veg, broccoli contains *sulforaphane*, an agent that scientists believe helps fight against cancer.

**Cabbages** are usually classified by the shape of their heads and by their color. My favorite is the pointy heads because they look like coneheads from *Saturday Night Live*. Like broccoli, most cabbages prefer cooler weather and can even handle a light frost at the end of the growing season.

**Brussels sprouts** are really just mini cabbages that form on a stalk. Instead of growing just one cabbage at a time, in the same space on a single stalk of Brussels sprouts you can grow 30 mini ones!

**Kale** is basically a wild, leafy type of cabbage. Gardeners love it because it is easy to grow, can handle cold temperatures and is pretty cute to look at! It also packs a vitamin punch, with lots of calcium, potassium and vitamins A and C. Many types of kale are available, but all of them basically grow the same.

## Sunlight

Traditionally, broccoli loves the sun, but it definitely needs a little shade as well, as it can quickly turn yellow with too much heat. If you live in a hot climate, look for varieties specifically grown to handle the warm temperatures.

Cauliflower is the same as broccoli when it comes to all things EXCEPT that the cauliflower loves the heat . . . just not the sun. Smart gardeners tie the leaves of the cauliflower plant together overtop of the head to prevent it from getting too much sun and turning ricey. (Ricey = bad and grainy.)

Cabbage and Brussels sprouts need some cool weather to really form good, tight heads. Like kale, plant them in an area that gets morning sunlight but has some afternoon shade.

Kale prefers cooler weather, so plant it in a section of the garden that gets a little midday shade.

### Dirt

Brassicas love a rich soil with lots of nutrients and mulch. Also consider adding some fine fireplace ash to the soil to help lower the acidity, as these plants are prone to a fungal disease called *clubroot*, which happens when the soil acidity is too high.

### Space

Brassicas take up a lot of space in a garden, which makes them a bit of a challenge for condo owners or container gardeners. Each seed needs to be planted 2 feet apart in the row, and each row needs to be 3 feet apart. So basically, 12 plants take up the same square footage as some bachelor apartments. If you are worried about space, choose plants that are dwarf varieties, or try the sprouting version of broccoli, because you can harvest from one plant repeatedly, unlike the classic options, which are "one and done."

### Plant

To get a jump on growing, you can start your brassicas indoors 4–6 weeks before you plant them in the garden. If you are strapped for indoor space, planting seeds directly in the garden works well too. Make sure to give your larger-growing varieties of broccoli, cauliflower, cabbages and Brussels sprouts lots of space to grow. Keep the seeds at least 12 inches apart. Do the same for large-headed kale, though some of the new varieties can be treated like lettuce and planted closer together.

### Care

Brassicas need lots of moisture to grow. Keep them well watered all summer long, especially during the hottest months. When the soil temperature gets too high, brassicas can develop the "yellows," which is a yellowing of the leaves from root rot. If this begins to happen, add lots of mulch around the bottom of the plant to keep more moisture in the ground and to keep the roots cooler.

Cabbages are also prone to worms that burrow into the plant and live on the inside, eating the tender leaves. Keep an eye out for round holes going into your plant and treat the plant with a product called *Bt* (*Bacillus thuringiensis*), which is a helpful bacterium effective in getting rid of these worms.

### Harvest

Harvest your brassicas when they get to the size that you would like to eat. Just remember, with Brussels sprouts, you can start harvesting the larger sprouts from the bottom of the stalk, allowing the smaller ones near the top more time to grow. Once you harvest the cauliflower and cabbage heads, the plants are done and can be removed. With broccoli and Brussels sprouts, leave the stems in place, as they will often grow side shoots, which can be harvested later in the season.

Make sure that you don't start to harvest kale until it is at least 60 days old. If you start cutting the leaves before the roots get established, you will slow down the plant's growth. (Older leaves on a kale plant are tough and stringy, so you don't really want to eat those anyway!) A good rule of thumb is to keep at least six of the

old leaves around the bottom of the plant and harvest the inner leaves up to but not including the crown. Kale tastes better after a good frost. Because it is a cold-hardy plant, make sure to keep some leaves on even after everything else has been removed from the garden.

### Prepare for Next Year

Most brassicas will not overwinter in cold climates, with a couple of exceptions. Many of the kale varieties are hardy enough that they can regrow after being completely frozen. Try leaving a few in the ground over the winter. Come spring, if the stalks are firm and still have some color in them, odds are that they will send up new shoots.

# Carrots

PLANT DIRECTLY IN THE GARDEN
IN EARLY SUMMER

{ FULL SUN }

**Want an easy plant to grow?**
Go for carrots! They are a perfect plant to try with kids because carrots are so simple and forgiving. You can pretty much stick the seeds in the ground and get some form of this vegetable. The key is to use good soil! Orange carrots are relatively new to the gardening scene. Try growing some of the vintage varieties that include reds and purples. Just don't be surprised when you slice into them and the inside is very different than the outside.

**Sunlight**
Full sun all day long makes for a sweeter carrot packed with lots of vitamins A and C.

**Dirt**
The ONLY thing that carrots really need is loose and sandy soil so that they can grow nice long roots. The looser the soil, the straighter the carrot. This is because it doesn't have to grow around the clumps. Make sure that they have at least 10 inches of good soil to grow in. Even in your backyard, you'll want to till or "fluff up" the soil so that the carrots can grow tall and straight. Crooked carrots are cute to look at but a terror to peel, cut or cook with.

Carrots like lots of compost in the ground, especially if you have sandy soil, which is often light on the nutrient side of things. Carrots grown in "rich" soil produce lots of extra roots and get hairy, which is

kind of gross. If this bothers you, don't give carrots any additional fertilizers.

**Space**
Traditionally, you want to plant your carrots at least 1 inch apart so that they get nice and big and have room to grow. But with "baby carrots" now so popular at the store, planting carrots close together and really packing them into a space has become more mainstream.

**Plant**
Plant seeds every couple of weeks for the first few months of summer. This is the easiest way to stage your harvest so that you'll have fresh carrots all summer long.

Soak the seeds in water overnight. This helps speed up the germination process and gets those babies growing faster! Carrot seeds are REALLY TINY! The goal is

to plant them 1 inch apart, but for most of us, that is virtually impossible. Instead, your carrots may have to be thinned (not like Jenny Craig thinned). Carrots don't do well when they are crowded in the row, but because the seeds are so-o-o small, it is easier to plant them and then pull out the smallest ones that are crowded together.

It's a bit of a *Hunger Games* moment when you must sacrifice some for the good of the others. Do your first thinning at the 4-week stage of life, and then once more at 7 weeks.

## Care

Be cheap on the watering. Carrots that get too much water will often split. (This is more common in the vintage varieties.) Less water might mean smaller carrots, but they will be all the sweeter.

## Harvest

Leave your carrots in the ground until you want to eat them. Even if they go through a frost, they will actually taste even sweeter, as the cold brings out the natural sugars! *Mmm-m-m-m-m!*

## Prepare for Next Year

You can definitely try to leave your carrots in the ground over the winter.

Unfortunately, carrots are biennials, which means they have to get through two summers before they will produce seeds, which you can use later to grow more carrots. Carrot seeds grow on tall stalks that are easy to cut off and save in a paper bag. To grow seeds, you'll need to put a few carrots in the root cellar or the basement, in a cardboard box full of clean wood shavings. Replant them in the spring and see if they will grow for you! If they do, don't harvest any of the seeds until they dry out on the stalks.

Growing cucumbers is my Achilles heel. If there is one crop that I have failed at more times than I'd like to admit, it's cucumbers, and that totally sucks because I love me a good pickle! Cucumbers should be easy to grow because they like a warm summer and lots of sun. Unfortunately, cucumbers do not like a hot summer and too much sun. Finding the right spot for your cucumber patch is the most important part of the process. The gardeners who have had success with their cukes are the ones who got it right when they picked their spot.

# Cucumbers

PLANT IN THE GARDEN WHEN
ALL THREATS OF FROST ARE OVER

{ FULL SUN }

## Sunlight

Lots of sun... but not too much. I like to pair my cucumbers with corn. The corn provides a little shade when the sun is at its hottest, and the cukes will happily grow around the base of the cornstalks without hurting them.

## Dirt

Cucumbers will grow in many soil conditions so long as the soil is warm! Add fertilizer or compost before you plant the seeds, and again when the plants are 3–4 inches tall.

## Space

Cucumbers need space. Make sure to give them some room to create vines and spread around the bed. I like to plant my cukes about 12 inches apart.

## Plant

Cucumbers are totally cold-phobic. Make sure to wait until all chances of frost are over before even starting your seeds or seedlings in the soil.

Mom says to plant on a hill or a mound and Farmer Bill says that this is a myth. Here is the truth: The mound helps with drainage for beginner gardeners worried about overwatering their cucumbers. Farmer Bill knows his shit and doesn't need a mound. (LOL!)

Cucumbers are a bizarre vegetable because they last longer when they are off the ground, even though the trailing vines are naturally designed to crawl all over the place. In nature, the cucumber fruit is the way the plant ensures its survival from year to year. So when it grows on the ground, it rots faster, ensuring that new

seeds get into the soil for the next growing season. This doesn't really work for us as gardeners. Instead, consider making a cucumber hammock (not to be confused with a banana hammock)—see DIY below.

## Care

The ideal condition for cucumbers is warm but not hot. Cucumbers that grow in hot conditions need a lot of water or they taste bitter. Make sure to give them a good soak every few days, but never let them stand in puddles. Cukes hate wet feet.

Cukes are the fav treat of lots of different beetles. Be prepared with your natural methods (see page 91) to stop the feeding frenzy. The good news is, at least you know where to check in the garden for bugs first!

## Harvest

If you get it right, cucumbers will keep producing all summer long; just make sure to keep harvesting them as the little cukes grow. A cucumber left on the vine will continue to take all the plant's nutrients and overripen, turning bitter and becoming inedible.

## Prepare for Next Year

Make sure to leave one or two good specimens on the vine until they turn yellow. This will allow the seeds inside to develop. Before the frost, harvest your yellow cukes and scoop out the seeds. Dry them and save until next year!

# Cucumber Trellis

Cucumbers are not the best climbers, so creating a vertical wall isn't going to work for them. Instead, your trellis needs to be on a slope so that you can help the vines grow up it:

1.  Start with a frame. Any type of four-sided flat structure will work. I've used old picture and window frames and they usually make it through at least one or two seasons. Just be sure that the frame is at least 3 feet × 3 feet.

2.  Cover the frame with a mesh, net or lattice. You need something that will allow the air to flow around the vines to help prevent rot.

3.  Bury the side of the trellis closest to the plant to help prevent the trellis from moving in the wind.

4.  Elevate the other side of the trellis about 3 feet into the air. This is the perfect slope for the cucumber.

5.  Plant a row of carrots or radishes under the trellis. (Why waste the space?)

# Eggplant

**Surprisingly, not a lot of** attention is paid to the eggplant, but when it comes to sexy vegetables, the eggplant is at the top of my list! It is actually a fruit, but that gets really confusing, so I'm going to call it "a vegetable that produces fruit." (Because that's not confusing at all.) I have a secret crush on eggplants, not because I love the flavor but because they are the first plant that guests always see when they visit my garden. I always get the "OOOOOH ... what is *that*?" question. Eggplants have great leaves and stunning flowers. This is probably why people include them in their flower gardens.

Eggplants fall into two groups: Asian, and everything not Asian. The two are the same in terms of growth and care, but Asian eggplants: have thinner skins; tend to be long and thin rather than short and stout (although I've seen lots of both); have fewer seeds, which makes them less bitter and have a more delicate flavor (sometimes called bland!). The second eggplant group used to be titled Italian, but now it's become American, Italian, Dutch ... and whatever country wants to stake a claim to a breed of eggplant. These eggplants are often bigger, thicker and in some cases more flavorful, able to stand up to a rich pasta sauce or deep-frying.

There has been some debate about male and female fruit on the eggplant. Some say that the male has an "outie" indentation at the bottom of each fruit, whereas the female has an "innie." The reason for telling the difference is that the female fruit tends to have more seeds, making it bitter. (If only it was *that* easy to detect a bitter person!) Botanists have long argued that there are no such things as male and female fruit on plants, so the debate continues.

## Sunlight

Full sun for these beauties. They need a long and hot growing season to really produce a lot of fruit.

## Dirt

Eggplants are not fussy when it comes to the soil that they will grow in. They care more about the heat.

### Space

For all the patio growers and balcony gardeners, eggplants come in minis that are perfect in small spaces. Otherwise . . . aim to grow your eggplants about 2 feet apart.

### Plant

Start your eggplants indoors to make sure you give them a head start. Like I said, they need a long growing season to really develop a full crop. Plant them outside 2 weeks after the last frost to make sure that the soil is good and warm. Consider covering them at night if it gets cool.

Eggplants need a stake or a tomato cage to support them, as the fruit can get heavy. All eggplants grow on a shrub, but the weight of the fruit sometimes makes them look like they are growing on a vine.

### Care

Once they are growing, don't give them anything except water. If you treat these plants too well, then you will get lots of leaves and very little fruit. Think *Fifty Shades of Grey* and you'll do well with eggplant, but beware: Like any jilted lover, eggplants can bite back . . . they have spines that really hurt.

Look for little orange eggs under the leaves of your eggplants. These belong to the Colorado potato beetle, which happens to love eating eggplants. Either squish the bugs or blast them off with the hose.

### Harvest

If you harvest fruit, more will grow so long as the weather is warm. Fruit are ready to be picked when they have nice coloration and firm and glossy skins that yield a little when pressed.

### Prepare for Next Year

Eggplants do have very tiny seeds that you can save. Let a fruit ripen until it is wrinkled. Cut in half to scoop out the seeds. Wash the halves to remove some of the pulp. Dry and save for next year.

# Fruit Trees

BEST TO START OUTSIDE
WITH YEAR-OLD SAPLINGS

{ FULL SUN }

**Every backyard needs at least** one fruit tree. But I've even seen condo dwellers successfully grow small trees in planters, so maybe I should have said every *home* needs a fruit tree! I inherited a few, and then added more because growing your own fruit is a big part of being sustainable in your own space and a great way to have fresh, chemical-free produce in your backyard. The one big issue with fruit trees is the mess. Rotten fruit on the ground can cause some garden hygiene issues, including wasps and rodents. Planting a fruit tree is definitely a commitment. Many varieties of fruit trees need to be planted with a friend of the same species nearby so that they will cross-pollinate (cherries are the worst for this). Having said that, new grafting techniques (adding a branch from one tree onto the trunk of another) have created trees with several different kinds of the same fruit growing on them. I have a pear tree that grows five different types of pears! They take up less space than an entire orchard and it eliminates the need for planting more than one tree for cross-pollinating.

## Sunlight

Full sun all the time is the only way to really get the best flavors from your fruit tree. When an apple, plum or any fruit ripens on the tree, the flavors are exceptional, but so are the increased vitamin and beneficial glyconutrient content.

## Dirt

Fruit trees grow best in sandy-loamy soil. They love a little shot of nutrients early in the spring and again when they are beginning to bear fruit. In a container, it is super important to make sure that there is great drainage. This is mandatory for any citrus tree because these trees absolutely hate sitting in water.

## Space

There are literally thousands of varieties of fruit trees, including dwarf and columnar (ones that grow vertically with only a few horizontal branches). When it comes to spacing, make sure to follow the directions for each individual tree. Generally, I like to plant my fruit trees 15 feet apart unless I am working with dwarf varieties.

## Plant

Fruit trees are extremely tough to grow from the seed stage (not impossible . . . just really hard). Most often, they are sold as year-old saplings online and from garden centers. When planting these in the garden or in a pot, make sure that you don't put them in too deep. If they came already in soil, only plant the tree to the existing height that it is used to. If you get your tree and it is "bare root" (no soil to be seen), make sure to plant only a few inches above the height of the last root.

The average fruit tree really begins to bear a full crop around 7–8 years after planting, sometimes even longer if they are in a container. Not to worry, though, if you are like me and lack patience. You will start getting fruit pretty consistently from year 3 onward . . . just not a lot.

## Care

Insects, bacteria and fungus all make their home in the grass and dead branches at the bottom of a tree. It's important to keep these areas clear so fewer pesticides and chemicals are needed on your fruit. To reduce the maintenance, make those trees look a little better and improve their health, try my lasagna cardboard-and-mulch technique (see page 22) around your fruit trees. The cardboard barrier removes other plant competition, like weeds, so that the trees get better access to water and nutrients. The cardboard and

the mulch also naturally break down into the soil, adding more food and effectively feeding your trees for significantly longer. As well, the dark-brown mulch around the trees helps to make them look like they belong, so that they are part of the landscape instead of an eyesore off in the corner.

When it comes to indoor trees or trees that go outside on the balcony for the summer, pay attention to little flying bugs around the soil or in the leaves. These gnats can be treated with insecticidal soap (see recipe on page 88).

## Harvest

Fruit trees are harvested when the fruit is ripe. The best way to determine this is to keep taste testing. Rock hard might be what you are used to at a grocery store, but those fruit are definitely not really ripe. The flesh should be soft and sweet and easily bitten into. There is, however, a magic window with fruit trees. If you leave the fruit on too long, it will start to get either "punky" or "mushy." (Neither of which is a good thing.)

## Prepare for Next Year

IMHO, the one crappy part of having fruit trees is pruning in the winter to ensure that the sap stays in the roots as opposed to in the branches. Pruning in the winter not only makes sure that your trees remain productive in future years but it also promotes the right kind of spring

growth. In the winter the trees are dormant, which means that all the life (sap) is protected below ground. With no leaves or fruit, you can clearly see the shape of the tree and what needs to change.

Here are my simple steps for pruning the classic apple or pear tree:

**Look for spurs!** Most of the apple and pear trees in colder climates produce fruit on short stems called *spurs*. These spurs need to be saved to ensure that you get lots of flowers in the spring, because it is the flowers that turn into the fruit ... which grow on the spurs! If you have a tree that has spurs, then you want to limit your pruning to one-third of last year's growth. On average, an apple tree grows 6–8 inches per year, so prune 2–3 inches off the ends. This type of trimming promotes more side shoots and even more fruiting spurs.

**Remove the suckers!** Also called *water shoots*, these are thin, pencil-like branches that grow from the older branches. You will often see them clustered around areas of previous pruning. These suckers will never provide fruit and need to be removed. They will also crowd the center of the tree,

preventing light from getting to the apples or pears below and slowing down the time that they ripen. Cut the water shoots flush to where they start but make sure to save them. They are great to use as plant stakes in the spring.

**Remove the old stuff.** There are instances where you have to remove some of the thick branches from older trees. At this time of the year, you can safely remove up to one-third of a tree's mature wood without causing problems. Branches that are cracked, have moss growing on them or are crossing and starting to rub are all signs that they need to come out. Remove the branch in sections with a large saw to keep them manageable. Remove the entire branch, all the way back to the bulge where it attaches to the tree.

The tricky part with container trees or ones that you've brought inside for the colder months is knowing when to prune them, because they never go dormant. I prefer to prune indoor trees in the winter months because the light levels are lower and the tree will not be going through a growth cycle.

**Garlic is one of those plants that** is an overachiever in your garden and is a must-have for several different reasons beside the obvious edible one. Garlic helps deter bugs and herbivores from chowing down on your tastier plants. To stop rabbits, deer, even cats, plant garlic around the outside of your beds and planters. The animals will smell the garlic and avoid everything growing deeper in the garden.

# Garlic

Most of the garlic we use today comes in two varieties: hardneck and softneck. Hardneck garlics send up a flower stalk called a *scape*, which needs to be removed (and eaten: see my Grilled Garlic Scape Pesto recipe on page 181) before the plant will develop the bulb below the soil. Softneck garlics do not usually send up a flower and they grow a bulb with many smaller cloves.

## Sunlight

Garlic grows as soon as the garden thaws out, so full-sun locations always do best because snow melts there first! Garlic can handle some shade as well, growing in and around other plants. This often promotes lots of green leaf growth, but sometimes stunts the size of the bulbs.

## Dirt

Garlic is fantastic at adapting to any type of soil. If you continue to harvest and replant some of your cloves, the garlic will completely adjust to work in your type of soil. Some even say that the flavor gets better every year because of this adapting process.

## Space

Garlic can be grown in any garden or container space. To get a great big bulb, plant your garlic cloves about 2 inches apart to let them get established.

## Plant

Garlic for eating needs to be planted in the fall, preferably when the ground is cold to the touch but not yet frozen. Don't be too worried if you start to see green shoots before the snow sets in. Garlic will often correct itself and start to regrow in the spring.

Planting garlic is easy. Every single clove in a head of garlic (the little sections

in the big one) can grow into a plant. You can literally get the garlic from the grocer and plant it in the ground and it will grow. Plant your garlic cloves in a grid of 2 inches × 2 inches away from the next clove. You don't have to be exact here; planting like this just helps the garlic grow bigger. Plant each clove about 3 inches into the ground, and slightly deeper in windy locations so that the stalk is stronger, with a better anchor.

## Care

Beyond snipping off the flower shoot in early summer, garlic needs very little care. Other than my pet chickens, nothing seems to even touch garlic, making it pest-free in the garden. You don't even need to really water garlic, unless you have a long drought; then 2 inches of water per week will help your garlic grow bigger.

## Harvest

Garlic will produce two different edible crops. The first, scapes, are the cool curly flower structure that is seen usually in June. Cut these off about 3 inches from the ground where the stalk starts to get woody. These scapes are like a garlic version of chives (see my Grilled Garlic Scape Pesto recipe on page 187). After you've harvested the scapes, put a reminder in your calendar that the garlic bulbs will be ready in 3 weeks. Once the entire plant starts to dry out, it's time to harvest the bulbs by literally pulling them out of the ground. *Dead easy!*

## Prepare for Next Year

Make sure to place your extra garlic in a cool, dark place to dry out until you are ready to use ... or plant again! Putting garlic in a paper bag to overwinter will also help keep the bulbs dry. Any moisture can cause fungus and mold.

Most of the herbs that we grow for cooking and flavor are Mediterranean by descent. They grow best when you can re-create their favorite growing conditions: hot, sunny and sandy! Turn the page for my Top 10 Herbs to try.

# Herbs

PLANT ALL YEAR ROUND;
PERFECT FOR POTS

{ FULL SUN }

## Sunlight

Most herbs love sun. If growing on a windowsill, north-facing windows are the hardest to grow on because they get the least amount of sunlight. Use the sunlight test on page 8 to see how much sun you really have in your windowsill. Just make sure to do this test again in the winter months when we get considerably less light. Good herbs for low-light situations are lemon balm, chives, oregano, mint, parsley and thyme.

## Dirt

Herbs love sand! If you are repotting or trying to grow in a container or planter, add some sand to the soil mix. By blending the sand with the other soil, you improve the drainage. Aim for 1 part sand to 2 parts potting mix. If you are planting in the garden, make sure you have a well-drained space. Most herbs originally grew in rocky-sandy soil.

## Space

One of the first spots that a future gardener often starts with is with herbs on the windowsill. If you can keep these alive, you can pretty much grow anything! Unfortunately, it's not as easy as you think. *Duh!* There are hundreds of great herbs that are easy to grow, so if you didn't have success with the windowsill, consider trying containers on the patio, vertical gardens or even mixing in herbs with your flowering perennials. There is definitely an herb for every growing situation in your home.

## Plant

Herbs love holes! Say what? If herbs are planted in a pot, they MUST be in a pot that has a hole in the bottom. They hate sitting in a puddle of water. If you have a really cool planter that doesn't have a hole but you want to put an herb into it, then keep the plant in its original pot, put gravel in the new planter, put the old pot in the new one and cover it with moss so that no one knows!

# TOP 10 HERBS

| Herb | Favorite Conditions | Pros | Cons |
|---|---|---|---|
| Basil | Full sun, well-drained soil. | This herb likes it hot! Lots of sun, lots of water and a pot with holes in the bottom is all it really needs. | Harvest often! If basil goes to seed, it stops producing the yummy leaves. When in doubt, pinch off the tops. |
| Chives | Sun or semi-shade. | The easiest herb to grow. Chives are the first one up and the last one to bed in the growing season. | These plants can spread! Beware of chives taking over your garden with new plants starting from roots off the mama plant. |
| Cilantro | Does best with some shade from noon to 3 to prevent it from going to seed. | The green shoots are the cilantro. When the hot summer weather hits, you get seeds, which are called coriander. It's a two-for-one herb! | Doesn't like to be moved. Find a good spot and let it grow. Don't bother starting indoors. |
| Dill | Loves the sun! Happy dill can grow up to 6' tall. | Super forgiving herb. Needs very little from you once it's in a sunny space. | Beware of the seeds. Dill likes to spread everywhere. If you don't stay on top of it, you can have a dill forest pretty quick. |
| Mint | Sun or semi-shade is best. Needs 6 hours of bright light per day and regular watering. | With thousands of varieties and so many new flavors, there is a perfect mint for everyone. | Super aggressive in the garden. Beware planting this outside of a container. |
| Oregano | Does best with little attention or fertilizer. Plant in part to full sun, water sparingly and enjoy! | Both the Mexican and Mediterranean varieties are easy to grow and taste amazing. Plant this with your veggies, as oregano is a great companion plant. | Keep an eye on it! Some varieties will spread fast through your space. If it does, just rip it out and dry it for winter use. |
| Parsley | Parsley is a biennial herb, which means it grows for 2 years before you need to replant. Choose a warm, sunny spot with well-drained soil. | Great in containers on the patio or in pots in the garden. | Not so good in the house, as it needs lots of sun to stop it from going floppy over the sides of the pot. |
| Rosemary | Grow in containers. Loves the heat. Find it a happy spot and leave it there. | Nearly impossible to kill. | Doesn't like to be moved, which makes it tough to bring in for the winter. |
| Sage | Medium soil, medium light and medium water! Sage doesn't have any special needs. | Loves other plants! Put it in a planter with other fragrant plants like oregano and rosemary and enjoy the smell all summer long. | No real negatives—just stay away from fertilizers, and remember that too much food makes it taste bland. |
| Thyme | Bring on the heat! Thyme loves lots of sun and very little water, making it perfect for rock gardens. | Simple to grow and easy to spread, thyme can be split over and over to fill lots of areas in the yard. | Make sure to choose a variety specifically for food. Many of the ground cover options have no taste . . . at all. |

Not all herbs love the same size of pot. (Which kinda screws with the whole uniform look on the windowsill.) Some herbs, like parsley, prefer a deep pot that allows for longer roots, whereas others need a wide pot for lateral root growth. The rule of thumb: Tall plants like tall pots and bushy herbs like wider pots.

Growing herbs outside is basically the same principle as on the windowsill, with a few exceptions. Many herbs (like the evil mint plant) spread underground with small rootlets. When you grow these plants in a pot, you effectively contain those running roots. In the ground, however, they can take over the entire garden bed. I like to plant my herbs in a pot . . . in the ground. I usually work with a pot that is larger than the one I bought the herbs in, so that they get a little room to grow. I plant my mint in this bigger pot using the same system as planting an indoor herb garden. Then I dig a big hole and plant the new pot into the ground so that the soil surface in the pot is the same height as the soil around the outside. If you don't like the way the plastic pot looks in the garden, simply raise the plant inside so that you can bury the pot even deeper. *Easy!*

Many herbs can be super aggressive in the garden. Plan on planting most of your perennial herbs in a larger pot directly in the garden so that the roots don't invade your space.

Also, insects don't usually go for the strong smells of most herbs. Plant lots of them around your more sensitive plants like cucumbers and tomatoes. They act as a smell camouflage, hiding the sensitive plants from bug devastation.

### Care

Whether indoors or out, when it comes to watering your herbs, most of them are drought tolerant and prefer to be watered less. Once a week is plenty for most herbs, but for a little more guidance in knowing when to water, consider planting a rosemary bush in your mix. Rosemary is a great indicator plant: When the leaves start to droop or look wrinkled, it's time to

between the pot and the window. Keeping the roots warm will go a long way to keeping your plant happy. When they are outside, full sun in a warm and sheltered space makes for happy herbs.

### Harvest

Most herbs are used for their leaves, so as soon as there are a lot of leaves, you can begin to harvest some for your cooking, teas or medicinal purposes. Just make sure never to harvest more than one-quarter at a time, so that the plant can regrow throughout the season. At the end of summer, you can either bring your herbs indoors, or you can completely harvest the remaining leaves and compost the plant.

### Prepare for Next Year

Many herbs will produce seeds that can be harvested to start new plants the following spring. Basil is a classic example, sending up lots of tiny seed-covered branches toward the end of summer. There are also many type of perennial herbs that will overwinter even in the toughest of conditions. Plants like mint, sage, rosemary and thyme seem to thrive on neglect. Just be careful that they don't spread through your entire space.

If you decide to bring your herbs indoors, don't be surprised if they start to lose leaves. This is pretty common as they adjust to lower light levels.

water everyone! For a pot that is 4 inches across, put 6 tablespoons of water on top of the soil once a week. For every extra inch of width, add 1 more tablespoon. *Simple!*

Herbs love airflow! (No... not high winds, more like gentle breezes). The movement of wind around the leaves not only strengthens the plants it also helps prevent diseases like powdery mildew and fungal infections.

Herbs also like heat! Keep them warm in the winter if they are beside a window that is drafty or cold to the touch. The easiest way is to use a blanket or a thick towel

When all else fails, you can always grow lettuce. (And that's a good thing!) Lettuce is so easy to grow and has so many varieties you can create your own salad blends all summer long. There are hundreds of types of lettuces, but most fall into three categories: *Head lettuces* form rosettes in the center of a collection of leaves. *Leaf lettuces* grow individual leaves instead of clusters. *Romaine lettuces* grow long tall heads, as opposed to the shorter rosettes of a head lettuce. These plants are known for their thick ribs. Although arugula and spinach are definitely not lettuces, they grow the same way and can be treated with the same rules.

# Lettuce

## Sunlight

The more heat, the more bitter your lettuce becomes. If you are growing lettuce on a rooftop or a patio and it gets blasted with full sun, consider putting it behind a taller plant or in a shadier corner so that it gets a break from the heat. Of all the lettuces, romaines are best suited for hot temperatures.

## Dirt

Lettuce can tolerate all kinds of soil but does best with lots of fertilizer in a well-drained situation. I love to mix all kinds of lettuce in pots on the balcony or around the deck.

## Space

The type of lettuce that you choose totally determines the spacing that you need. Leaf lettuces can be planted tighter together in a neat and compact row, whereas the head lettuces need extra space to really fill out: often 8–10 inches apart. Lettuces are a great container or planter option, as they happily grow alongside every other plant and can be jammed into a tighter space and still do well!

## Plant

Most lettuce prefers to be grown in cooler temperatures, so plant lots in spring and fall. For the advanced gardener, *succession planting* is a way to have lettuce all summer long. There are a few ways to do succession planting. One option is to start in spring by planting only varieties of leaf lettuce. Then a few weeks later, plant

romaine, and then some head lettuce toward the end of the season. Another option is to plant a single row of each variety to start, then add a second row of each variety 10 days later. By staggering the planting time, you don't end up with everything ripe and ready at the exact same time. Trust me, I love salad . . . but even I can't handle salad for every meal.

## Care

Lots of water for lettuce. It needs a regular soak to keep those leaves growing big and beautiful. Water when the soil on top of the bed or container starts to look cracked or dry.

Keep an eye out for small tunnels going through the outer leaves of head lettuces. This is a good indicator that a worm may have crawled into the middle of your lettuce for a snack. *Eww-w-w-w.*

## Harvest

For leaf lettuce varieties, you can begin to harvest once the leaves reach about 2–3 inches tall. Harvest the lettuce every single day to keep fresh and tender shoots growing. Head lettuce needs to be left alone for a longer period before harvesting so that the actual "head" can form in the middle of the plant.

Many leaf lettuce varieties are referred to as "cut and come again." (Worst name ever!) This means that you can continually harvest from the plant until the end of summer, provided you always leave a few

small shoots to form. Just make sure to keep an eye on these, as they like to *bolt* (think Usain Bolt). Arugula and spinach especially go from a healthy leaf ready to harvest straight to seed mode so fast that your head will spin. Keep harvesting the older leaves to prevent the seed stalks from forming. Once a lettuce or spinach starts to go to seed your harvest is significantly reduced. If your lettuce sends up a stalk with flowers on it, it's time to plant some new lettuce because yours is getting ready to go to seed. If you have the space, let the seeds develop and save them for next year!

## Prepare for Next Year

Lettuce is a very easy plant to collect seeds from. Once the seed stalks have begun to dry out and easily snap in half, it is time to remove them and the plant. Save the seeds by trimming off the stems/seed pods and shaking them into a labeled envelope for next spring and start all over again!

**Even if onions happen to be**
the cheapest vegetable at the
market, growing your own is
wickedly important for several
reasons, including keeping pests
and insects out of your garden!
I also get pumped about onions
because they are the very first seed
that you can start indoors, so I grow A LOT
every year. When choosing your onion seeds (or
*sets*), look for long-day and short-day in the description.
Long-day onions are better suited to the north, where the daylight hours are longer,
than in the south. This is important because the length of daylight impacts how
a bulb or globe onion grows.

# Onions

## Sunlight

Long-day and short-day onions have different light requirements. Onions are shallow rooted, which means the roots that they grow stay near the surface. Add a layer of mulch around your plants to help the roots stay hydrated in the hotter months.

## Dirt

Onions like a loose soil that is full of composted goodness. They prefer to grow in soil that has been really turned over and worked so that it is free of clumps and is light and airy. They also love a little ash! They are huge fans of phosphorus and potassium, so adding wood ash or bone meal will help them grow.

## Space

Onions are a great pest deterrent because they are so fragrant. I plant onions throughout the garden in circles and in rows around the other vegetables that could use a little defense. Just make sure to keep them away from your beans and peas! Spacing of onions is totally based on the type you choose. *Globe onions* (onions with large bulbs) need more room, whereas flat onions need less.

## Plant

Growing onions is relatively easy. Throw a bunch of seeds on top of a soil-filled take-out container and wait for the little shoots to start growing. Just make sure to provide lots of light and lots of water, and to put a hole in the bottom of the container so you

have lots of drainage. When the ground warms up, gently pull the small shoots apart and plant in a row. Done!

Globe onions often need a longer period to grow. Which is why they are often sold as little onions already started, called *sets*. Planting these is similar to planting garlic (see page 124), except you plant them in the spring.

### Care

Make sure to keep the onion rows free from weeds. Onions hate competition. You can also be a little generous with the watering for onions. Those shallow roots make it hard for onions to access much water below the surface. I like to give my onions at least 1 inch of water per week using a rain gauge (see page 65), and a bit more during the really hot months.

### Harvest

Globe onions can be harvested when the aboveground stalks begin to turn yellow or dry out. This signals that the onions have stopped growing. For green onions, scallions and chives, you can begin to cut and eat the tasty shoots as soon as they are up and out of the ground. Add lots of these tangy shoots to your food for a pop of flavor!

### Prepare for Next Year

Several varieties of onions are perennial in most climates, meaning they regrow every spring. For others, treat them like garlic (see page 126) and store several bulbs in a paper bag in a dark, cool space over the winter. Plant them in the garden the following spring!

While these plants can be identified by the color of the flowers or the way they grow, most of us really only care about the harvest and buy our seeds based on the result. Here are the types of peas that you can shop for:

# Peas

PLANT DIRECTLY OUTSIDE
AND PLANT EARLY

{ FULL SUN }

## Varieties

**Shell peas** are the ones where the outer casing is removed before eating. You have to wait to harvest these plants until the peas inside are nice and plump!

**Snap peas** are eaten with the outer casing, but when the inside peas are filled out. Several of these varieties are now being sold as "stringless," which means that they don't have the fibrous vein running along the backside of the pod that has to be removed before eating.

**Snow peas** you see A LOT in stir-fry. These flat peas are used for the pods and not for the peas inside. I'm a fan of the Royal Snow, which is a purple variety. (*Kewl!*)

## Sunlight

Peas do best in full sun. Some of the climbing varieties can easily get over 8 feet long in search of more sunlight. Make sure you provide something for them to climb on so that they can access more sunlight.

## Dirt

Peas love well-drained garden soil and do well with a bit of ash or even bone meal to add a little extra potassium. Avoid using compost that contains pine needles or coffee grounds because of the increased acidity, which peas totally hate.

Peas are a special plant because they put more into the soil than they take out. Peas encourage the growth of a type of bacteria that adds nitrogen to the soil, making it better for other plants to grow in. I will often plant carrots and radishes near my peas to take advantage of the richer soil.

## Space

For climbing varieties, sow your peas about 1 inch deep and 3–4 inches apart. For dwarf or bush peas, make sure to leave at least 18 inches between your plants so that they get lots of sun and airflow to keep them healthy.

## Plant

Peas are one of the earliest vegetables to harvest in the garden, so planting them first just makes sense because you can plant other stuff once they are harvested! Because peas like it cold, they can be planted as soon as the soil can be worked.

The perfect planting situation for peas is to have the roots in the shade and the shoots in the sun, which makes peas ideal on a balcony or patio where the railing shades the planter/pot. Just make sure that you have a trellis or something vertical for any of the climbing varieties because they love to grow up instead of out!

And make sure to plant your pea seeds directly outside because they hate to be transplanted.

## Care

I pack mulch around the plants to help keep the cold and moisture in the soil longer. Peas need to be kept well watered but not obsessively so. If the ground looks dry, give them a drink.

The one thing that is important with peas is to make sure that you move them around the garden. Peas have a long list of fungal and bacterial diseases that affect them. By rotating them around your space from year to year, you can help prevent the spread of these diseases from year to year.

## Harvest

Pick your snap and shell peas when the pods are big and plump and the peas inside have developed. Snow peas should be harvested before you start to get large peas inside the pod.

## Prepare for Next Year

Leave some peas on the vine or plant until they completely dry out and turn crunchy. These can be stored until next season and planted again!

Growing peppers has been a bit of a buzz for a long time as more growers try to kick up the heat and blow each other's taste buds off. For the home gardener, peppers are a great addition to any space because they are so easy to grow.

# Peppers

START INDOORS 8-10 WEEKS
BEFORE THE LAST FROST

{ FULL SUN }

Peppers are divided into two categories: sweet and heat (also called *bell* and *hot peppers*), though they are similar to grow and care for. Today's peppers also come with a spice measurement called the *Scoville scale*. This number lets you know how much physical damage you are going to do by eating the pepper. For example, a bell pepper has a Scoville number of zero, whereas the jalapeño comes in somewhere between 2,500 and 10,000. The newest varieties like the Carolina Reaper pepper have a Scoville measurement of 2,200,000. People who have eaten these peppers say that the burn is unlike anything you've ever experienced. (I'll take their word for it . . .)

## Sunlight

Peppers are considered tropical or subtropical plants. They love the sun. They grow as shrubs in the heat of the south but can't handle frost. In northern climates, peppers are grown outdoors as annuals, but some gardeners have had success bringing them indoors if they get enough direct light (12–15 hours per day minimum).

## Dirt

Peppers do well in average soil, whether in the garden or in a container. During the growth period, when the plant is producing leaves and branches, fertilize with nitrogen-rich products. Avoid adding too much, though! Overfeeding causes your plant to grow lots of leaves . . . and not a lot of anything else!

## Space

There are many, many, many types of peppers. Some are dwarf and some can grow huge, upward of 6 feet. When choosing your peppers, make sure to pay attention to the size of the plant so that you will know if it is suitable for your space.

## Plant

When growing peppers at home, start

indoors 8–10 weeks before the last frost and then transplant them outside when all threat of cold weather is over. Peppers can handle being transplanted and most varieties stay pretty compact, so you can grow them inside easily. By starting them inside, you can extend the growing season, which is very important for most pepper varieties because they take so long to mature.

Baby peppers like warm feet, so many home growers will place the planting tray on top of a heating blanket set at low. Once the pepper has developed several leaves, lowering the room temperature to 59 degrees Fahrenheit while keeping the heating blanket on will help encourage more fruit from the plant.

When transplanting, it is very important to plant your pepper in the ground at the SAME HEIGHT as it was in the pot. This is the one requirement that your pepper has. Otherwise, put it in a hot and sunny spot and let it grow.

Flag your hot peppers! Many gardeners have handled hot peppers with bare hands and then rubbed their eyes (or scratched their face… speaking from experience). Getting any of the chili oil on your skin is very painful. In fact, expert hot-pepper gardeners will wear rubber gloves when gardening around their pepper plants.

## Care

Your peppers love heat and humidity. Keep the soil moist around the roots with regular watering and a healthy layer of mulch to prevent drying out.

When your pepper plants are about to flower, spray them with Epsom salts (1 Tbsp to 4 cups of water). This shot of magnesium will encourage more fruit growth.

### Harvest

Unripe peppers are green. You want to harvest yours when they begin to change color. Make sure to use snips to remove the fruit from the plant to encourage more fruit to grow in the same spot.

## Prepare for Next Year

Saving seeds from peppers is easy! Just leave a few fruit on the plant until the skins start to get wrinkly. Remove the seeds from the fruit and dry them out on a paper towel for a few days.

Just make sure to get everything off the plant before frost hits, or you will have mush instead of peppers.

# Potatoes

START INDOORS IN A PAPER BAG

{ FULL SUN }

**Spuds are a food staple all around** the world . . . partly because of the flavor but also because of how easy they are to grow. They are a very abundant crop that can be started with just one small potato. I'm a huge fan of pretty colors when it comes to the potatoes I like to grow. Varieties like Russian Blues, which have dark-purple skin and blue flesh, and AmaRosas, which have red skin and flesh, are ALWAYS in the mix for me. You can plant an assortment of your favorites and some new types in the same potato planter.

## Sunlight

Potatoes need a lot of sun to develop lots of tubers from the original seed potato. The leafy greens above the ground need full-sun exposure, whereas the tender tubers below the soil need to be constantly covered to protect them.

## Dirt

The best soil for potatoes is a sandy mix that is light and well drained. As the plants grow below the ground, heavy clumps or clay make it tough for them to produce a huge crop. I like to add lots of compost and organic matter to my beds to ensure the plants have a lot of available nutrients, which helps them grow bigger.

## Space

Ordinarily, potatoes are grown in long rows with mounds of soil continually dumped on top of them throughout the season. To get a large crop, you would need a large section of the yard. This is pretty tough to do when it comes to a small backyard, and virtually impossible on a patio!

New growing methods have begun to reduce the amount of square footage you need, making it easier to get a large harvest without a massive resource commitment (see my DIY Vertical Potato Planter on page 145).

## Plant

To get your potatoes started, place them whole in a paper bag in a warm, sunny window for 2 weeks. As they start to grow little shoots, you can section up the tubers, ensuring that a root is growing in each section. Each one of these rooted spuds will turn into a full plant!

When planting potatoes in a trench,

make sure to dig it at least 6–8 inches deep. Plant your potatoes 10 inches apart in the trench. Start your next trench 28 inches away from the first one.

## Care

As the green shoots start to grow, add soil around the plant, burying at least 3–4 inches of the plant. This extra soil is where the new tubers will grow, so it is important to pack the soil in to protect them from the sun.

Keep your potatoes moist, but don't over-water them, as too much water will wash the mounded soil away from the tender tubers. During the hot months, consider adding mulch to keep the ground from drying out.

Potatoes have a lot of natural pests, including leaf hoppers and the Colorado potato beetle. Keep an eye out for chewing and damage on the leaves of your spuds. If you see signs of insect damage, start with insecticidal soap (see page 88) to help deter insects from your crops.

### Harvest

As the plants start to flower, you know it is time to check for baby potatoes, often around 50–60 days from when you planted them. Harvest carefully, making sure to get all the little ones. I prefer a pitchfork for this because I always split my taters in half with a shovel.

### Prepare for Next Year

Potatoes keep well in cold storage or a root cellar. Never store your potatoes near apples or onions, as the ethylene gas that they give off will cause your potatoes to sprout. If you do get sprouts starting on your potatoes, save them and plant these in the garden next season!

# Vertical Potato Planter

For the past few years I have been messing around with a type of 4 × 4 × 4 vertical potato planter that grows spuds in a smaller space. Here is my simple DIY that has had some amazing results!

1. For a 4 × 4 × 4-foot planter, you'll need 4 posts and a bunch of boards for the sides (depending how high you want to build it). Start by cutting 4 pieces of solid wood (like 4 × 4s) into 4-foot lengths to make your vertical posts for the 4 corners. Next, cut some boards for the sides, also in 4-foot lengths. You can use any food-safe wood (see page 26 for types of wood).

2. Build 1 side of the planter: Lay 2 of the posts on a level surface and attach a few of the side pieces, starting at the base. Repeat this process so that you have 2 sides of your box started. Your side walls need to be at least 6 inches tall to start, but not more than 1 foot.

3. Stand up the two side walls and attach them together with more of the horizontal wood pieces to create a shallow box with 4 posts sticking out of the corners. (You might need a friend for this.) Place the whole planter in its final location—you're ready to start prepping to plant!

4. Add at least 6 inches of good soil in the bottom of the planter.

5. Spread a layer of seedling potatoes in your planter 1 inch deep in the soil, leaving 5 to 6 inches of space around each one. The best potatoes to plant are the ones that already have little shoots started, so either buy them that way or put your own in a paper bag in a warm window for a few weeks to get them going. Cover your potatoes with more soil and water well.

6. As your potatoes start to grow, add another layer of side boards onto your planter. Add more soil around the small plants, leaving a few inches of the plants exposed.

7. Keep repeating this process as your potato plants grow, building the planter higher and adding more soil. Every time you add a layer, it will encourage little spuds to grow at each spot.

Growing pumpkins is easy, but growing gigantic show-stopping pumpkins . . . now *that* is a challenge. The keys to growing any pumpkin or winter squash (same same) are pretty straightforward as long as you do them all. Pick a good line of seeds. Pumpkin genetics are key to giant pumpkins. Which is why competitive growers won't share the seeds from their biggest specimens. Big pumpkins produce big pumpkins!

# Pumpkins

PLANT 160 DAYS BEFORE HALLOWEEN
FOR THE BIGGEST PUMPKIN
ON THE BLOCK!

{ FULL SUN }

## Sunlight

Pick the absolute sunniest spot in your yard/garden. This is really important because the leaves of each vine need to produce enough energy to grow 3–4 pounds of fruit weight. (That's a lot of energy!)

## Dirt

For the best pumpkins and squash, well-drained soil that is packed with nutrients works best. By bulking up on compost and fertilizers in the fall, you can ensure that the good stuff is present BEFORE you plant the seeds. My secret is to stick a large dead fish in a hole 2½ feet below the surface of where you want to plant the pumpkin. The fish will break down in the soil over the winter, adding a hit of nutrients just when your pumpkins need them the most.

## Space

Pumpkins need a lot of space, as their vines can grow up to 10 feet long . . . in several directions. If you are limited in space or want to grow these in a container, look for bush varieties of squash, which stay relatively compact.

## Plant

Pumpkins need around 160 days of growing time to really grow huge! If you are aiming for Halloween or for the local pumpkin-growing contest, count backward 160 days to see when you should start your seeds. Pumpkins can be sown directly into the garden once the soil is warm and the frost threat is over, so for most northern regions, this means starting seeds indoors first. I plant mine inside around the end of April. There is one major issue with starting early, though: Pumpkins hate to be moved or to have their roots disturbed. This makes it

really tough to transplant them when the soil has warmed. I recommend a fiber or compostable pot that can go from inside to outside without upsetting the plant. Plus, go slow and be gentle!

### Care

Water lots, but only at night! Pumpkins grow in the evening and this is when they need the most watering. An average giant pumpkin needs 20 gallons of water per week, spread between two waterings. Also, make sure to water at the roots, avoiding the leaves, to help reduce fungal growth.

Add liquid calcium, but make sure to follow the instructions on the bottle. Plants need calcium to help absorb other nutrients, like nitrogen, from the ground. By adding store-bought soluble calcium, your pumpkins can absorb lots of nutrients, and more nutrients means bigger fruit!

If you want to grow one huge specimen, remove all but the biggest baby pumpkin as the fruit begins to grow. This is important to ensure that all the food the plant produces goes to one spot!

You can also start many plants from your original seed group by planting the vines. Everywhere that the leaves connect to the vine forms a "knuckle." By lightly planting these knuckles in the soil (while still attached), you generate a second growth of roots, which will help feed a giant pumpkin.

Cover the pumpkin. Shade on your pumpkin is really important in preventing it from ripening too soon. When a pumpkin is exposed to dry heat and sunlight, it begins to form a thick skin to protect itself. This skin restricts how big the pumpkin can grow. Uncover the pumpkin 1 week before showtime if you're aiming for a big one, to ensure that it ripens.

### Harvest

Many squash can be harvested when they are young and small, keeping them tender. A squash/pumpkin will continue to grow until the skin becomes hard and waxy looking. A simple test to see if your pumpkin is still growing is to break the skin of the fruit with your fingernail. If it is tough and you can't break the skin, odds are the fruit has reached maximum size. I like to let my fall squash stay in the garden as long as possible before the first frost.

### Prepare for Next Year

Save the seeds from all your squash and pumpkins by scooping them out of the fruit and drying them out on newspaper in the sun. Once the remaining flesh is dry, you can remove it from the seeds and put the seeds in a dark, dry place until spring.

# Radishes

PLANTING DATES VARY (EARLY SPRING
TO EARLY FALL) DEPENDING ON
THE TASTE YOU'RE LOOKING FOR

{ FULL SUN }

**In every garden there is** *always* **room for radishes! These little gems are the easiest vegetable to grow ... and one of the fastest to produce. I usually have five or six on the go at various stages of production.**

## Sunlight

Radishes need lots of sun, but heat makes them spicy. Plant these in an area where they can get morning sun but are protected from the intense heat of early afternoon.

## Dirt

Radishes need loose soil. Consider planting them with your other root vegetables in a bed that has been worked to remove any of the rocks or clumps.

## Space

You can do rows of radishes, grow them in planters and flowerpots and mix them in with almost any other vegetable combination, making them ideal for maximizing every square inch of your available growing space.

## Plant

Some radishes can mature in less than 35 days, which in the gardening world is damn fast! Every 2 weeks, I'll plant another group of radishes somewhere in the garden to fill the empty spots. Other radishes, like daikon, require a longer growing season.

For mild radishes, start growing them in early spring and again in late summer/early fall, as they grow well in cool temperatures. If you want a little extra kick, plant your radishes in hotter weather. The temperatures in June and July are perfect for adding some zing to your radishes ... just make sure to keep an eye on them and harvest before they start to get woody. Always keep sampling your radishes to know when they are at their best and when they are starting to get tough and fibrous. When they are no longer tasty, it's time to rip them out!

Most radishes are grown just like carrots, with seeds being planted in a row of shallow 1-inch-deep depressions. Lightly cover them with soil and gently water every few days until the seeds have started to grow. You may have to thin the radishes after 2 weeks to ensure proper spacing of

about 1–2 inches. Just make sure to save the little shoots, as they are amazing in salads as a microgreen.

## Care

Water your radishes lightly every few days until they get started. Once they are sprouting, water less often, but deeper to encourage good root growth. The key to growing good radishes is totally tied to the flavor you want. If you like your radishes more on the mild side, plant with lots of compost and water often. The extra water in their lives ensures that they grow faster!

There are lots of insects that like to eat your radish tops . . . especially flea beetles. The good news is that we usually don't eat the leaves. Don't panic if all the leaves have little circles chewed through them.

## Harvest

For salad radishes, harvest while they are relatively small and before they split . . . picture busting out of the front of your pants after a holiday feast! For daikon and fall radishes, leave them in the ground as long as possible, then remove them before the frost.

## Prepare for Next Year

Radish seeds are relatively easy to save, and because radishes grow so quickly, you can often get seeds in the first year. Once the seeds are dry and brown, cut the entire stem off. Put it and the seeds into an envelope for a few days. Shake the envelope hard to get all the seeds off the stem, then remove the stem and compost it. Now you have your seeds in an envelope for next year!

When I was a kid, berries were my favorite part of the garden because I could eat them off the bush! Even now as an adult, the thought of eating a strawberry that is warm and sweet from being in the sun is totally making my mouth water. In general, there are two types of strawberries: June bearing, which produce their fruit all at once (in June—*duh!*); and ever bearing, which will produce fruit all season long, no matter what the light levels are.

# Strawberries

PLANT IN EARLY SPRING

{ FULL SUN }

### Sunlight

Strawberries want to be in a sunny spot. Makes sense—the more sun . . . the sweeter the fruit!

### Dirt

Strawberries need a lot of water, so make sure to plant them in a soil that has good absorption. It's best to stay away from sandy soil when planting your strawberries, because it drains too fast. Instead, this is the one time that having clay in your ground is totally a good thing.

### Space

Strawberries are one fruit that almost anyone can grow, whether you have a garden or just a hanging basket. They are great at producing fruit in their first season, making them perfect for kids or adults with short attention spans! I add alpine strawberry bushes to my planters, pots and hanging baskets. They love to climb over the sides and dangle, sort of like ivy does. Not only do they look good with their little white flowers but they also have tiny fruit that are great in a salad!

### Plant

Strawberries are planted in early spring and will often provide you with fruit in the very first season. Every year afterward, a happy plant will spread, producing more fruit.

Strawberries want to be the star of the show, so make sure to keep them well weeded and away from any competition. The traditional method of planting strawberries is in long rows that are at least 3 feet away from each other so that you can walk in between them during harvest time. We now know that you can grow

strawberries in almost anything and still get fruit. *Score!* So add some strawberry plants to your edible hanging baskets as a trailing vine option.

Strawberries have an issue with boundaries. They ignore them. A healthy strawberry plant will send out runners to start other strawberry plants and eventually take over the whole garden. It's a fruit colonization program. These runners can be chopped off with a shovel or a lawn mower and not physically hurt the parent plant. (Emotionally is another story . . .)

### Care

Put straw under your strawberries. *Duh!* To grow big strawberries, you need lots of watering. Adding straw under the plant keeps the berries from getting muddy and helps control pests and weeds.

Be prepared to defend your berries! Ripe strawberries are a hot commodity with birds, squirrels, rabbits, small children . . . you name it. If you don't keep an eye on your crop, someone else will!

### Harvest

Based on the type of strawberry you choose, you'll have a general idea when the harvest will start. Once your strawberries do start to ripen, plan on checking them every day. If you don't, birds, chipmunks and pests like slugs will help you harvest.

### Prepare for Next Year

Strawberries like a little insulation to protect the tender roots that are just under the surface. Once the leaves start to yellow and change color in the fall, bury the entire strawberry patch in 2 inches of clean and dry straw. You can always find small decorative bales around Thanksgiving, or hit up your local pet store for bunny bedding!

# Tomatoes

START INDOORS FOR BEST RESULTS

{ FULL SUN }

**I love me some tomatoes! Hands** down, tomatoes are my absolute garden favorite. Nothing even really comes close . . . okay, maybe peppers . . . but I REALLY love tomatoes. Every year I grow about 15 different varieties in the garden and in planters. I even have tomato babies from last year popping up pretty much throughout the garden from tomatoes that I grew the year before. Serious *#tomatolove* in my life.

It is hard to compare the taste of a store-bought tomato with one that you grow on your own. This is because the store-bought version usually ripens in the carton as it is being shipped. Growing your own also means a big increase in diversity. When you go into a grocery store, there really are only about 7–9 varieties of tomatoes to choose from. We can point the finger at mass production or at the farmers who want to make a living, or even at the grocery stores themselves because they don't source more options for us, but the truth is, we are also partly to blame. We have a mental image of the perfect tomato, and it's usually red, round and free from blemishes. As cooks, we think we know what we like for pasta sauce, burgers, salsa or even salads and very rarely do we deviate from our favorite varieties of Romas and beefsteaks.

Want to push your food boundaries when it comes to growing your own?

Never choose a tomato based on its color! White tomatoes are truly special and get very little credit because we assume that they are not yet ripe. White varieties like Snowball and Cream Sausage are not only stunning but also often have low acidity, making for a smooth taste experience. Also consider trying greens, blues and blacks! Look for stripes and bicolor choices to add visual complexity to your salads. A few of my new favorite "lookers" are Purple Bumble Bee, Ozark Sunrise and Red Zebra.

Tomatoes are also not all perfectly round and smooth. Don't limit your selection to the shape of your tomato. Accordion or ruffled varieties are both the ugliest and most beautiful options I've ever seen. Whether bumpy, scabby or creased, the shape and surface doesn't impact the taste. In fact, one of the best flavors I tried was from a mottled variety named Scabitha, which had hideous raised ridges all over the fruit.

### Sunlight

Keep tomatoes in a warm, sunny spot. The more sun, the more fruit! You can grow indoors, but with less sun you won't get the bumper crop you are hoping for.

### Dirt

Tomatoes love nutrient-rich soil. Either add lots of triple mix into your garden or consider investing in nitrogen-rich options like fish emulsion or biofertilizers made from plants and kelp.

Tomatoes also love calcium. I save my eggshells to put around the bottom of the plants. As the shells naturally break down, they add calcium directly into the soil. *Cheap 'n' easy, baby!*

### Space

Tomatoes love heat and hate cold, so the key to growing good tomatoes is full sun and warm soil. But don't be discouraged if you don't have the perfect growing conditions in your space. There are more than 10,000 varieties of tomatoes, so you can find one that will do well in your situation no matter where you are trying to grow them.

### Plant

Tomatoes will produce fruit all summer long, but most homeowners start seeds indoors so that they have little plants to put in the ground to extend the season. Don't plant until any threat of frost is over. You can plant seeds directly into the ground, but in northern climates, the growing season is too short to really get a lot of tomatoes.

Almost all varieties of tomatoes (except for dwarf and determinate, which stay small) need to be staked. The wire baskets don't work by themselves, as the skinny little legs buckle under the weight of a big plant. Make sure to add a stake (or even two) when the plant is young and use a flexible and soft tie to attach them.

Everything seems to love tomatoes: bugs, blight, fungi. Plant your tomatoes at least 3 feet apart to allow for some space and airflow between them to help prevent the spread of bad things.

### Care

The hardest part of growing tomatoes is really managing the water. Too much or too little can impact the growth and fruit development. The way you water is also very important for minimizing fungal infections on the leaves and around the blooms. Best practice for watering tomatoes is consistency! You want to keep the soil evenly moist for the whole summer. I water twice a week, leaving the hose on each plant for 5 minutes to make sure that water gets deep into the soil. To avoid fungal infections, avoid watering from above the plant, so the leaves stay dry.

Mulch around the bottom of the tomato plant once it is in the garden. The mulch helps hold water in the soil through the hot period and helps prevent blight (a common tomato disease) from forming on your plants.

To deter insects, plant garlic bulbs near the base of your tomatoes so that the fragrant shoots will grow as the plant does. Sort of like a symbiotic relationship that keeps bugs from wanting to climb up and eat the tomatoes.

### Harvest

Harvest your tomatoes when they are ripe. Leaving them on the plant until they ripen not only intensifies the flavor but also helps pack the fruit with extra vitamins and all the good stuff! Make sure to remove the mushy tomatoes from the ground around the plant. As they rot, they attract insects and promote fungal growth that can later affect the plant.

### Prepare for Next Year

Tomatoes are one of the easiest vegetables that you can grow year after year simply by saving the seeds. All of the 'mater-experts' agree that a tomato that is grown in the same garden for several years in a row, through seed saving techniques, just tastes better because it has adapted to those conditions.

# Tomato Seed Saving

Want to save seeds like a pro? Here are the simple steps that I recently learned to grow your own heirloom tomatoes from scratch!

**1** Start with a squishy tomato from the farmers market or your local grocer. Riper tomatoes are easier to work with when trying to remove the seeds.

**2** Cut the tomato in half and, using your finger, start scooping the seeds into a jar with a lid.

**3** Once you have all the seeds scooped out into the jar, add a few tablespoons of water. Give the jar a little shake and tightly seal it. The bad seeds and the meat of the tomato will float to the top, while the good seeds sink!

**4** Put your jar in the window or on the fridge. (This next part is a little gross.) You are trying to promote mold! Fermenting your seeds helps to remove the jellylike casing from the seed so that it will keep longer.

**5** After 3–5 days, drain the smelly water from the jar, carefully saving the seeds that have settled on the bottom.

**6** Put these seeds out on your BEST china. (I'm not sure why, but they seem to know when you use the cheap stuff.) Once the seeds have dried out on your plate, they can be used right away or saved in a labeled envelope for up to 10 years!

# Tomato Hangers

Like strawberries (see page 152), tomatoes will grow pretty much anywhere, any way, even hanging upside down! There are some great benefits to flipping over your plant, including:

- 🍅 Easier to access the roots of the plant for watering and for adding liquid fertilizers.
- 🍅 Crawling bugs and slugs can't get at the plants.
- 🍅 No weeding required—there are no weeds.
- 🍅 Staking or tomato cages not needed; gravity does all the work.
- 🍅 Hanging baskets can be moved and rotated if one side of the plant is getting all the sunlight.

Hanging a tomato plant is simple:

1. Start by cutting a 4-inch-diameter hole in the bottom of a plastic pail. If you have it, use a saw designed for cutting holes in drywall for installing light fixtures/pot lights.

2. Flip the pail over and feed the roots of the tomato plant through the hole.

3. Inside the pot, gently wrap the roots in landscape fabric to stop the plant and the soil from falling through the hole when watered.

4. Fill the pail with container or potting-mix soil that is lightweight. Do not use soil from your garden, as this will get very heavy when you water the plant.

5. Hang the planter at least 4 feet off the ground to ensure that the plant doesn't drag.

6. Water well to keep the plant producing all summer long!

VEGETABLES:
RECIPES

*Cedar Plank Roasted Onions (recipe page 183)*

The best part of a vegetable garden . . .
is the vegetables! Fresh veggies are delicious
on their own, but they're also great baked,
grilled, in salads, pickled and more.
Here are a few of my favorite ways to enjoy
the produce from my own garden.

# PRESERVING

## Storing Fresh, Canning, Dehydrating and Freezing

The thing about growing vegetables is that if you are successful, you'll get more produce than you can eat. It's great to be able to go into your garden and pick something for dinner fresh from the ground, but those beans and carrots won't stay in perfect condition, waiting for you to harvest them. All gardeners have that "Holy Shit!" moment when they realize they have more food than they can deal with.

Preserving the food is a perfect solution, and it's half the fun, so I've included some ways that I preserve the produce from my own garden. The chart I've included is to steer you in the right direction for what to do with the veggies you've grown.

*Blanching* **means to quickly boil the vegetables for a short period, then immediately put them into a bath of ice water to stop the cooking process. Think of this as a pre-cook.**

**Storing fresh** means refrigerating or storing food in a cold, dry and dark place. Basements and root cellars are ideal for this; I know some people who have made it work in an insulated garage, but that's risky due to temperatures fluctuating throughout the year (warm temperatures promote bacterial growth (*eww-w-w-w*), which is something you definitely want to avoid).

**Canning** is a way to preserve food by storing it in an airtight jar. Usually, there is some sort of liquid brine that acts as a preservative to prevent bacteria from forming. Read more about this on page 171.

**Dehydrating,** which means drying food, is a huge trend right now. This process uses heat to remove the moisture from the foods, either by leaving them in the sun, baking them in the oven or using a dehydrating machine (a machine I love because it's pretty tough to fail with). The dehydrating process is a slow one, so be prepared to give it several hours to work. The process brings out more flavor in your veggies, and certain veggies are definitely worth the wait—for example, the concentrated deliciousness of tomatoes that have been sun dried.

**Freezing** is really just shoving your food in the freezer in airtight bags. Ensuring that there is no air in the bag means that your veggies will last longer in the freezer without breaking down due to freezer burn. I'm an advocate of freezing individual vegetables, like peas, on a sheet pan for an hour first and then transferring them into an airtight bag. Doing this stops the food from freezing in a clump.

## VEGETABLE STORING

|  | Storing | Canning | Dehydrating | Freezing |
|---|---|---|---|---|
| **Apples** | For a while, but eventually they start to get soft, and who wants to bite into a soft apple? | In applesauce form . . . otherwise, they turn a gross brown color. | Yes, yes, yes! Dehydrating is the best way to store apples. Try adding a little cinnamon dust for some extra flavor. | I have a batch ready for a pie in the freezer right now. Just mix all of the ingredients with the apples before you freeze them. |
| **Asparagus** | In the fridge, stems in water for about 7 days max. | Definitely! | X | Definitely—blanch first. |
| **Beans (in pod)** | 3–5 days in the fridge. | Pickle them whole and serve them with cheese and crackers! | X | Definitely—blanch first. |
| **Beans (shelled)** | Can be stored for years in a dark, dry space in a jar or even a paper bag. | Can be preserved in oil or salted water. | Definitely! | Definitely—blanch first. |

| | Storing | Canning | Dehydrating | Freezing |
|---|---|---|---|---|
| **Beets** | Root cellar or fridge, 2 months. | Pickled beets work! | Can be done, but stains everything in the process. | Great for freezing. Fully cook first and then peel. |
| **Broccoli** | 4 days in the fridge. | X | X | Definitely—blanch first. |
| **Brussels Sprouts** | Root cellar, up to 5 months. Up to 2 months in the fridge. | Yes. | X | Not really. |
| **Cabbage** | Root cellar, up to 5 months. Up to 2 months in the fridge. | Definitely! (Love my sauerkraut!) | X | Not really. |
| **Carrots** | Root cellar, 6 months; or 2 weeks in the fridge. | Definitely! (Add a hot pepper in the jar . . . makes them sweet and spicy!) | Yup. Dried slices are a great addition to soups. | Definitely! |
| **Cauliflower** | 5 days in the fridge. | Definitely! | X | Definitely—blanch first. |
| **Celery** | Root cellar, 2 months; or 2 weeks in the fridge. | Definitely! | X | Definitely! |
| **Corn** | 5 days in the fridge. | Mini ones are doable. | X | Remove from cob—blanch first. |
| **Cucumbers** | 7 days in the fridge. | Uh . . . pickles are cucumbers. | X | X |
| **Eggplant** | Will keep in the fridge for several weeks but gets bitter with age. (Don't we all?) | Pickled works. | X | Blanch first and remove as much air from the bag as possible. |
| **Herbs** | 3–5 days in the fridge. Best if the stems are kept in water. | Make a pesto and THEN can them. | Of course! | I like them best when frozen in an ice cube tray in a little olive oil. |
| **Kale** | Store in the fridge until it goes limp, about 7 days, wrapped in wet paper towel. | X | Kind of like a dry kale chip. Grind to add to smoothies. | Chop first, then blanch before freezing. |

|  | Storing | Canning | Dehydrating | Freezing |
|---|---|---|---|---|
| **Lettuce** | Eat it now! Lettuce has a very short shelf life. | Eat it now! | Eat it now! | Eat it now! |
| **Onions and Garlic** | Root cellar, 6 months. Store in a breathable container or a cloth bag. | Definitely! | Yes—grind into your own onion or garlic powder for sauces and recipes. | Minimal success . . . they get mushy fast! |
| **Peas** | 1–2 days in the fridge. | X | Great in soups but need to be rehydrated before eating. | PERFECT! Blanch first. |
| **Peppers** | 1 week in the fridge. | Definitely! | Pepper powders are great for thickening soups! Dehydrate and grind. | X |
| **Potatoes** | Root cellar, 6 months. Store in a breathable container or cloth bag but not near onions or apples. | Try pickling with salt and vinegar overnight and then frying (so good). | X | Of course! That's how I buy my French fries! |
| **Pumpkins** | Best kept in a cool, dark place. | Puree them into a soup before you can them. | X | Yup. Roast them as 2- × 2-inch cubes until soft and then freeze. |
| **Radishes** | Store in the fridge for up to 10 days. | Love pickled radish on a burger. Pickling can tame a spicy radish. | X | Blanch first in little pieces. Freezing changes the structure and makes them mushier. |
| **Strawberries** | Only for a week, tops. | Works well as a jam or even a jelly. | Totally. So great in trail mix. | Yep . . . save them for your smoothies. |
| **Tomatoes** | Never in the fridge! They lose their flavor. Keep them on a counter or sunny windowsill and eat soon. | Yes! Make sauce! | Yup. (See tomato powder recipe on page 182.) | They can be frozen as a sauce or a ragout . . . the skins break down otherwise and you end up with mush when you thaw them. |

# Carson's All-Purpose Pickling Recipe

MAKES 2 CUPS OF BRINE

**Pickling is one of the easiest** methods of preserving your food. Although cucumbers are the standard, and I love them, there are lots more vegetables that can be pickled (see the chart on page 167–169). I like to play with the flavors of the brine I use, and you can mix and match my ingredients to create your own flavor profiles. The basic brine recipe is a pretty standard salt-sugar-water-vinegar equation: Just adjust the amounts as you need to suit the jar you are using, always keeping the ratio the same. (Before you start, make sure to read Preserving Safety on the following page).

**Brine** (adjust the amounts to suit the size of jar you are using)

1 tsp pickling or coarse salt

1 tsp white sugar

1 cup cold water

1 cup white vinegar

**Flavorings**

**Add before boiling:**

Allspice (ground)—1 tsp

Cardamom (ground)—1 tsp

Chipotle or ancho chili powder (ground)—1 tsp

Curry powder—2 tsp

Fennel seed (ground)—1 tsp

Garam masala—1 tsp

Turmeric (ground)—1 tsp

**Add whole to the jar:**

Cardamom pods—5 per jar

Celery seeds—up to 2 tsp per jar

Cinnamon sticks—1 per jar

Coriander seeds—up to 2 tsp per jar

Cumin seeds—up to 2 tsp per jar

Fresh dill fronds—1 per jar

Fenugreek seeds—up to 2 tsp per jar

Fresh garlic cloves—at least 1 per jar

Mustard seeds—up to 2 tsp per jar

Pearl onion—1 or 2 per jar

Black peppercorns—up to 2 tsp per jar

Hot peppers—1 per jar, but feel free to go hotter

Star anise pods—1 per jar

Fresh turmeric—3 dime-sized slices per jar

Mix all the brine ingredients together in a saucepan and add any "before boiling" flavoring that you fancy at this stage. Bring to a boil and boil for 1 minute.

Place your vegetables into sterilized jars and add any "add to the jar" flavorings that catch your eye. Fill the jars with brine up to ¼ inch from the top. Place sterilized lids on top and finger-tighten. (*Finger-tighten* means snug, but not as tight as the lid can go. You don't want to crank the lid too much because you need the air to escape from the jar.)

At this point, you can either boil the jars for 20 minutes to ensure an internal temperature of 240°F (see Preserving Safety below) or place them directly into the fridge, where they can be stored for up to 2 months.

**Preserving Safety** **Fresh food goes bad fast, and most veggies are water based, which doesn't help to slow down the rotting process. There are a lot of microorganisms that are perfectly happy living in rotting vegetables, including molds and bacteria. By preserving foods, you are stopping the harmful stuff from forming in the first place.**

**Sterilizing jars and lids before you fill them is an important step in reducing contamination. To sterilize, boil in a large pot of water for at least 10 minutes. Remove to a clean surface to let cool. Let dry and use within 24 hours.**

**Canning is a way to remove the air from the food, and it works to stop many microorganisms except the bacterium that causes botulism. Once a food is canned, it is really important to use a hot-water bath to raise the internal temperature to 240°F. Before you close the jar, add an acid (like vinegar or pickling mix) to kill any remaining bacteria that somehow snuck in. I like to add 1 tablespoon of lemon juice to the top of my preserves after I fill the jar, right before I boil the jar to seal it.**

# Asparagus with Pomegranate and Burrata

SERVES 4 (AS A SIDE)

**There is nothing quite like the** taste of asparagus paired with a tangy drizzle and the creaminess of good cheese! I love to serve this dish because of its bright, contrasting colors. Try it outside on the patio.

12 medium-sized asparagus spears (about ¼ inch thick), cut in half

1 tsp lemon juice

1 tsp olive oil

1 tsp salted butter

½ pomegranate

1 ball (9 oz) burrata cheese

4 Tbsp balsamic vinegar

Sea salt

Place the asparagus on a plate or in a flat, shallow bowl, drizzle with the lemon juice and olive oil and toss gently to coat.

Heat a large cast-iron or nonstick frying pan over medium-high heat and melt the butter. Reduce to medium heat and add the asparagus. Cook for about 6 minutes, or until the asparagus is softened. Remove from the heat.

Remove the pomegranate seeds and juice from the pomegranate by turning it over in a bowl and smacking it firmly with a large spoon. (Yeah . . . smack it good!) Make sure to save the excess juice.

Place the burrata in the center of a serving dish and slice off the topknot so that the cheese starts to run down the sides. Place the hot asparagus directly on and around the burrata and sprinkle with pomegranate seeds.

Put the pan back over high heat, pour in the balsamic vinegar and leftover pomegranate juice and boil for 1 minute. Drizzle over the burrata and asparagus and sprinkle with a few pinches of salt.

# Grilled Beets with Feta and Apple Mint

SERVES 6 (AS A SIDE)

**Grilling is one of my favorite ways to** cook beets because the smokiness of the barbecue paired with the earthiness of the beets is a match made in heaven. If you don't have a grill, roasting the beets at the same temperature in an oven works well too.

12 beets, anywhere between golf ball and tennis ball size (assorted varieties or just stick with your favorite)

1 Tbsp cooking olive oil

½ cup cubed or crumbled feta, room temperature

6–8 mint leaves, chopped (apple mint is one of my fav varieties for this recipe)

Balsamic vinegar, for drizzling

Pinch of fleur de sel or flaked sea salt

Preheat your grill or oven to between 385°F and 400°F.

Remove the leaves from the tops of the beets. Do not peel or slice. Place the whole beets in a bowl and coat with the olive oil.

Grill or roast the beets for about 20 minutes, turning halfway through, until a fork will easily go into them.

Remove from the oven and let cool enough that you can handle them. It's okay if the beets cool completely, but they are better when slightly warm.

Slide the beet skins off by hand. They should easily slip off with a little pressure. Just make sure to wear rubber gloves for any of the red beet varieties, as the juice stain is brutal to get off your hands.

Chop the beets into bite-sized pieces or serve whole. Mix the warm beets with the cheese and mint so that the cheese starts to melt, coating the beets in a creamy rich sauce. Transfer to a serving plate and drizzle with the balsamic vinegar, just enough to add some zing to the dish. Sprinkle with salt and serve!

# Kale Pesto and Poached Egg on Toast

## (with Optional Avocado)

**This is truly the breakfast of** champions! I love the way the tanginess of the pesto punches up the fattiness of the avocado with a lemony zing. Add the richness of a medium-poached egg and you have mouth nirvana!

## Kale Pesto

Kale pesto is a way to get your family to eat a superfood without any of the high-pressure sales tactics.
Truth is, the fam probably won't even notice that it's kale. I prefer to make this using a bright-green and leafy variety of kale, as opposed to a dark leaf, so that the pesto stays a vibrant color (instead of looking like sludge).

**MAKES 1 CUP PESTO**

2 cups fresh kale, woody part
    of the stems removed

½ cup fresh basil leaves

½ cup toasted walnuts,
    almonds or pine nuts

½ cup grated Parmesan cheese

2 Tbsp fresh lemon juice

½ teaspoon salt

½ cup extra virgin olive oil

If the kale is a chewier variety, blanch for 30 seconds in hot water before proceeding.

Place the kale, basil, nuts, cheese, lemon juice and salt in a blender or food processor. Pulse 3 or 4 times just to get the chopping process started.

Slowly add the olive oil while blending at high speed. Keep an eye on the thickness of your pesto. If it starts to look runny, stop adding olive oil. If it is too thick, add more oil to adjust. The pesto will keep for 2 weeks in the fridge in a sealed jar; or freeze for up to 6 months.

## Poached Eggs

The perfect poached egg is a decadent thing, even more so when it comes right from your chicken coop. Everyone always talks about the dark-orange yolks from free-range chickens, but for me it's the freshness that makes the difference. I love to have these on toast with my kale pesto for either breakfast or as a midday snack.

**MAKES AS MANY EGGS AS YOU LIKE**

Egg(s)
White vinegar
Coarse salt

Crack the egg(s) into individual cups, being careful not to break the yolk(s). Splash a touch of plain white vinegar in each cup.

Bring a large pot of salted water to a boil (add 3 Tbsp of coarse salt for every 5 cups of water). Once the water is boiling, give it a hard stir so that the water is spinning in one direction.

Slowly pour each egg out of the bowl and into the center of the water vortex. You can do this in batches of 3 or 4 depending on the size of your pot. Immediately turn off the heat, leaving the eggs to cook in the hot water. Timing will vary, but 4½ minutes usually does the trick for a large egg to get firm whites and a runny yolk. Remove from the water using a slotted spoon.

### To serve

1 slice of toast per egg
Flaked salt, for serving
Avocado (optional)
Lemon juice (optional)

Put a generous schmeer of kale pesto on a thick slice of toast and top with a perfect poached egg. Don't forget to add a healthy pinch of flaked salt on top! For a variation, add some sliced or mashed avocado and a splash of lemon juice.

*Harissa-Glazed Carrots (recipe page 178)*

*Grilled Garlic Scapes (recipe page 181)*

# Harissa-Glazed Carrots

SERVES 4 (AS A SIDE)

I'm a huge fan of sweet and spicy, especially when it comes to changing up a traditional staple vegetable like a carrot. Harissa is a spicy paste from North Africa made with chili peppers, herbs and garlic. I pair it with the sweet from local maple syrup for a taste explosion!

12 six- to eight-inch carrots (assorted varieties, but preferably all the same size)

2 Tbsp olive oil

5 star anise pods

2 cinnamon sticks

1 Tbsp maple syrup

1 tsp harissa (or more to jack up the heat)

Finishing salt

Clean and peel your carrots, then blanch them in a pot of boiling water for 3 minutes.

In a cast-iron or heavy-bottomed frying pan, warm the olive oil, star anise pods, cinnamon sticks and carrots over medium heat. Cook until the carrots begin to caramelize, about 6–8 minutes, turning occasionally to ensure even browning.

Remove from the heat. Discard the cinnamon and star anise, then add the maple syrup and harissa and toss to coat. (Adding the maple syrup to the pan with the harissa means the heat will evenly blend the two ingredients.)

Serve warm, adding salt to taste just before the carrots hit the table. You can keep the pan warm in the oven (175°F) until ready to serve.

*Photo on page 176*

# Mom's Pink Applesauce

MAKES 3 LARGE JARS
(ABOUT 12–15 CUPS)

I'm a bit of an applesauce snob. Probably because I grew up on an apple farm and got to eat it freshly made by my mom every fall. A few things to mention . . .

**Not all apples are created equal.** Sour apples make a tart sauce, so unless you want to add a lot of honey, skip them! The sweeter the apple, the less honey you need to add.

**When exposed to air, apples turn brown.** Some do it faster than others. If you have selected a type that browns fast, coat in a little lemon juice after slicing.

**Pretty pink sauce comes from red apples with their skin still on.** Specifically, apples from the Cortland family. My mom's favorites are Red Corts (if you can find them). Including their skin has nutritional value too, as the skin provides almost half their fiber content and increased amounts of vitamins A and K.

5 lb organic or homegrown Red Cortland apples (or any variety with deep-red skins, such as Empire)

2 Tbsp lemon juice or naturally occurring ascorbic acid (optional)

2 Tbsp pure honey (add more if you are working with a tart apple)

Wash the apples, then cut into quarters. Core the quarters, then cut each one in half. Coat with lemon juice, if using (you can skip the lemon juice with any apples from the Cortland family, as they don't brown).

Place the apples into a large lidded pot or Dutch oven. Add ¾ cup of water and cook over high heat until the apples puff up, about 5 minutes. Make sure to stir from time to time to prevent the apples from sticking to the bottom of the pot.

Process the cooked apples into a bowl through the smallest disk of a standard food mill. The food mill will catch the skins and smooth out any large chunks by grinding them up. (You could also use a food processor for this but you will need to remove the skins first.)

Stir in the honey, to taste. If you did not use lemon juice, you have the option of sprinkling in ascorbic acid according to package instructions. Mix well.

Eat immediately or get canning! To can: Fill sterilized jars with applesauce, leaving ¼ inch at the top. Place on the lids and finger-tighten. Boil the jars for 20 minutes. Remove from heat and let cool. Check the lids to ensure that they are still tight and that you can't push down on the top to create a pop. These jars of sauce will safely last up to 6 months in a cool, dark space.

**Ascorbic Acid** Ascorbic acid helps to prevent fruit like pears and apples from turning brown. It acts as a color stabilizer and antioxidant, and can also help prevent microbial growth, keeping food fresh longer. It is available at most large grocers carrying baking and pickling supplies.

Grilling garlic scapes over high heat mellows their garlic flavor. It also adds sweetness by charring the natural sugars in the plant, which works wonders in this delicious pesto. Add this pesto to fresh pasta or your favorite tomato salad for an unforgettable flavor experience.

# Grilled Garlic Scape Pesto

MAKES 2 SMALL JARS

12 fresh garlic scapes

2 Tbsp plus ¾ cup extra virgin olive oil

3 Tbsp lemon juice

½ tsp salt

½ cup grated Parmesan cheese

¾ cup roasted unsalted pistachios

Preheat your barbecue to 450°F.

Lightly coat the scapes with the 2 Tbsp of olive oil and 1 Tbsp of the lemon juice.

Place the scapes directly on a hot grill and cook for 30 seconds on each side, or until char marks begin to appear.

Place the warm scapes into a blender or food processor and add the salt, Parmesan cheese, pistachios and remaining lemon juice. Pulse 3 or 4 times on high speed just to get the chopping process started. Slowly add the remaining olive oil while blending at high speed. Keep an eye on the thickness of your pesto. If it starts to look runny, stop adding olive oil. If it is too thick, add more oil to adjust.

For a variation on this recipe, try adding a jalapeño to the grill with the scapes or switching out pistachios for toasted pine nuts. To preserve its great green color, freeze any unused pesto until needed.

*Photo on page 177*

# Oven-Dried Tomatoes with Thyme and Garlic

MAKES 12 TOMATOES WORTH (SEE NOTE)

**Here is my fav recipe that takes** the flavor profile of the dried tomato up a notch. Use these on salads, or pulverize the tomatoes, garlic and herbs in a blender to make tomato powder, a perfect gluten-free thickener for stews and sauces. Just be sure to slice the tomatoes consistently. The thicker the slice, the longer it takes to dry out, and thin slices are very brittle and can crumble easily.

THE AMOUNT THIS RECIPE MAKES DEPENDS ON THE SIZE OF YOUR TOMATOES AND HOW MUCH WATER IS IN THEM. BIGGER, JUICIER TOMATOES SOMETIMES YIELD LESS THAN A FIRMER, MEATIER TOMATO.

12 tomatoes (any variety bigger than a cherry tomato)

2 heads garlic (about 20 cloves)

Salt and pepper

12 sprigs of a woody herb (thyme, oregano or rosemary all work well)

Preheat the oven to 325°F (you can also make these in a dehydrator, which takes about the same time).

Slice the tomatoes about ⅛ of an inch thick. (If you can stand the slices up on their sides, they are too thick and will take forever to dry out.) Line 2 sheet pans with parchment paper and spread the tomatoes out on top.

Peel the garlic cloves and chop them in half. Scatter the cloves around the tomato slices, and season sparingly with salt and pepper.

Place in the oven and bake for 2 hours. Remove to flip the tomato slices and lay the whole-herb sprigs across the tomatoes. Return to the oven for at least 2 more hours—for tomato powders you want them crispy, whereas some chewiness is good for chopping and putting in salads.

Remove from the oven and let cool. Use the tomatoes slices whole, or pulse them for several seconds on high speed, along with the garlic and herb leaves from the pans, to make tomato powder. Both the slices and the powder will keep for years in a sealed mason jar stored in a cool, dark place.

I love the flavor of smoke—in fact, I'm a fan of anything that you can make taste like a campfire. And if you can partner that smoky goodness with the natural sweetness of root vegetables, you have a winning combination. Roasted onions are perfect when paired with the charred smokiness of a cedar plank off the grill.

# Cedar Plank Roasted Onions

MAKES 6 ONIONS (AS A SIDE TO ANY GRILLED MEATS)

1 cedar plank, ¼–½ inch thick × 12 inches long

2 Tbsp salt, plus extra for finishing

6 large onions (any variety will do, so long as they can sit upright)

Olive oil, for drizzling

2 tsp honey or aged balsamic vinegar

Fresh parsley, coarsely chopped

Start by soaking your cedar plank in water for at least 1 hour, or even better, overnight. To do this, place it in a bucket full of water or in the sink with a weight on top to keep it from floating. Season the water with the salt, to promote the absorption of water into the cedar and to enhance the flavor of the plank.

When ready to grill, preheat your barbecue to 425°F.

Cut the tops and bottoms off your onions and drizzle the remaining chunks with olive oil. Place the onions on the plank and put the plank on the barbecue. Cook for 25–30 minutes, or until the onions are soft and golden. Do not move or turn your onions while they are on the plank.

Remove from the barbecue, drizzle ½ teaspoon of honey or balsamic vinegar over the top of each onion and let rest for 7 minutes. Serve warm or chilled, sprinkled with a little salt and some fresh parsley.

*Photo on page 164*

VEGETABLES: RECIPES

# Paper Bag Peppers

**If you have any luck at all with** your pepper plants, you'll have more peppers than you need at any one time. There are lots of ways to preserve them, but one of my personal favorites is to roast and peel them. Baking, grilling or just burning the hell outta the skins is the perfect way to break down the fibers of the pepper (making them soft) and to bring out the natural sugars, making them a sweet treat in your savory dishes. Use these in salads, on burgers or anywhere you want a healthy pop of flavor!

You can roast peppers in the oven, on the flame of a natural gas stove or even on the barbecue. You are effectively using a heat source to burn the skins and to cook the flesh . . . without scorching the good stuff!

Peppers (spicy or sweet)

Olive oil

Salt and pepper

If making these in the oven, preheat the oven to low broil. If using the barbecue, preheat it to 425°F.

Core your peppers, removing the stem, seeds and pith (the white part). Cut them into either halves, thirds or quarters (your choice, based on the size of your peppers) and rub olive oil on the inside and outside.

Next, it's key to get your peppers as close to the heat source as possible. If doing them in the oven, place your peppers on the top rack, directly under the broiler. Blast them with heat for 3–8 minutes, depending on how hot you can get it; or until they are soft and nicely charred all over.

Remove the peppers from the heat and toss them into a paper bag. Seal the bag and steam the peppers for 15 minutes.

Using your hands, slide the skins off the cooled peppers and season with a little salt and pepper. Store these in the fridge submerged in olive oil; or preserve them in a pickling brine by following the canning instructions on page 171.

# Buttered Radishes

SERVES 4–6 (AS A SIDE)

**Butter and heat do amazing** things to radishes! For this recipe, I love to use a good-quality salted butter. Even if you have spicy radishes from the garden, the cooking process with the butter mellows their flavor and brings out the natural sugars in these root vegetables. This recipe also works well with herbs like thyme, tarragon or rosemary if you want to vary the taste.

25 assorted radishes

3 Tbsp salted butter

2 Tbsp dried thyme leaves or 3 Tbsp fresh

Finishing salt, to taste

Preheat the oven to 375°F.

Cut off the stems and the roots from your radishes and chop them into bite-sized pieces so that they roast evenly.

Heat an oven-safe frying pan over medium-high heat, add the butter and melt until it starts to sizzle. Add the radishes and cook for 4–6 minutes. When they start to brown, stir once and then transfer the pan to the oven. Roast for 15 minutes.

Remove from the oven and stir once more to ensure that nothing is sticking to the pan. Sprinkle with thyme and salt, to taste. Serve hot.

# Savory Strawberry Salad

SERVES 4–6 (AS A SIDE OR APPETIZER)

**This sure-to-please salad is a** combination of firm strawberries still warm from your sunny garden, paired with the licorice flavor of Pernod, a French liqueur. If you're afraid of the black licorice flavor, don't be—the natural juices of the strawberries smooth out the anise flavor of the Pernod. I love to pair this salad with anything off the grill or bring it to a potluck to impress! Tart and sweet, with a kick of black pepper and the freshness of shredded basil, the dish is a winner for dinner.

2 dozen plump strawberries (beware of strawberries that are overripe; the alcohol will turn them into mush)

2 Tbsp good-quality olive oil

8 fresh basil leaves, torn or cut into chiffonade (see note)

2 Tbsp Pernod

Cracked coarse black pepper, to taste

Trim and quarter the strawberries and place in a bowl.

Drizzle with the olive oil, then add the basil and mix evenly so that each berry has some fresh basil on it. Drizzle the Pernod over the top.

Season with pepper, to taste.

**To chiffonade basil, flatten and stack the leaves, then tightly roll the stack like a cigar and slice it into ribbons.**

# Tomato Panzanella Salad

SERVES 6 (AS A SIDE OR APPETIZER)

**I LOVE ME SOME TOMATOES!!!**

I love mixing all the varieties of my homegrown tomatoes in one salad so that each bite is a little different. A good panzanella (tomato and bread) salad is the perfect way to wow guests with a rainbow of colors and flavors. I use a dense, chewy bread like a sourdough that can soak up the tomato juices.

1 loaf of bread

½ cup good-quality extra virgin olive oil

3 garlic cloves, minced

4 cups mixed chopped tomatoes (with juices!)

1 cup chopped parsley

1 large cucumber, cubed or sliced

1 medium sweet onion, chopped

½ cup cubed or crumbled feta, or 1 Tbsp flaked sea salt

Preheat the oven to 325°F.

Cut the bread into 1-inch cubes and toss in a bowl with half the olive oil and the minced garlic. Distribute the cubes onto a sheet pan and bake for 35 minutes, or until cubes start to brown on the edges. Keep an eye on the minced garlic; if it starts to brown, take everything out. Let cool.

Combine the tomatoes, parsley, cucumber and onion in a large bowl. This mix should be wet from the tomato juices. Add the baked bread cubes and toss well.

Garnish with either feta cheese or flaked salt. Let the panzanella rest at room temperature for at least 30 minutes to allow the bread to soak up some of the tomato juices.

CHICKENS

Dreaming of having a flock of your own?
This chapter will help make your dream
a reality by showing you the truth
about backyard chickens (and why chicken
sweaters are never a good idea, even
though they're so damn cute).

# CHOOSING CHICKENS

So you think you want chickens? I'm with you on this one. I love my girls! Have a read of the info that follows first, though, to determine if keeping chickens is something you can truly commit to—there is a lot a prospective chicken parent should know, and this information is a perfect way to help you decide if you are ready for a 10-year commitment!

It's important to check first whether you are allowed to have chickens in your space, be it your own backyard or a shared condo rooftop. City and building bylaws are getting pretty tight on this subject. As more homeowners have become urban chicken farmers, the number of complaints from neighbors has risen every year. Some cities have specific rules—for example, coop placement in relation to property lines; hens versus roosters; the number of chickens you can own—and may require you to apply for a permit.

## Chicken Breeds

When I talk about chickens, I'm talking about the egg-laying birds; meat birds (or broilers) are another subject altogether. Raising chickens for meat is a whole different ball game, and after trying my hand at 100 broilers, I can honestly say that I'm never going there again!

Deciding on the right breed of egg-laying chicken is like deciding on the right type of puppy to get or car to drive. There are so many variables. Before you start shopping, ask yourself the questions that follow, take note of your answers and then look at the details of the different breeds listed to find your ideal match.

1. How cold is it during the winter? Do you need birds that can handle colder temperatures? (Some have feathered feet to help them stay insulated.)
2. How many eggs do you want per day and do you prefer fewer larger-sized eggs or more smaller eggs? (Some chickens will lay multiple small eggs a day, whereas others will just lay a really big one every few days.)
3. Do you want your chickens to be able to fly? (No joke. Some chickens, like bantams, can get some good height, which is great for avoiding predators but a pain in the ass when it comes to building high fences to keep them secure.)
4. What color of eggs do you want? (Brown chickens tend to lay brown eggs, but there are lots of other options out there. Blue eggs are a personal favorite because they make me think the Easter bunny has been in the coop fooling around with the chickens!)
5. How friendly do you want your birds? (Some breeds are more affectionate than others, which is great if you want to interact with them. I've also found that the friendly birds will pretty much follow any stranger they latch onto.)

And here's the info on my favorite breeds of chickens. Most of these are pretty common in most regions, with a few more unique breeds added because of their popularity among breeders and hobby chicken enthusiasts.

# CHICKEN BREEDS

| Breed | Pros | Cons |
|-------|------|------|
| Araucana | Prettiest blue-green eggs ever! Do well in both hot and cold climates. Can have some funky feathers around their heads, which give them a "just out of bed" look. | Not great breeders. Many of the chicks die in the egg, so if you want to have babies, it may take several tries to be successful. |
| Brahma | Big chickens that lay big brown eggs! Easygoing and play well with others. Best birds for colder climates because of their feathered feet. | Not good in the heat. These are some of the largest hens and roosters and can't fly more than a few feet. |
| Leghorn | Great for hot regions but can get frostbite in the cold. Lay beautiful white eggs. | Not the bravest birds. Tend to get stressed out in urban situations, causing lowered egg production. These chickens can fly, so build a coop with higher walls or a roof. |
| Orpington | Very friendly birds that are easy to care for; can handle colder weather and do well with children. Lay brown eggs and are not known for their flying skills. | Average layers, about 180 eggs per year. |
| Plymouth Rock | High egg production, 200 brown eggs per year. Stunning feathers used for many purposes. Good for warm or cooler climates but will need some heat in the winter months. | Moody birds. One day they are happy—the next they go for your throat. Heavy birds without a lot of flying abilities. |

| Breed | Pros | Cons |
|---|---|---|
| **Rhode Island Red** | Lay A LOT of eggs, 250 per year. Do well in hot or cold climates. As heavier birds, don't fly well but lay large brown eggs. | Usually easygoing, but sometimes you can get a crusty group that will chase small children (no joke). |
| **Sumatra** | Love the heat and humidity. Perfect for rooftop life. Gorgeous feathers on the roosters. This is a rare breed that is making a comeback. | Low egg production at 100 per year. Roosters are notoriously aggressive, as they were once used for cock fighting in Indonesia. Can fly really well, too well sometimes (I lost one into the trees and couldn't get her back). |

## Roosters

When creating your bird family, you should think carefully about whether you want to include a male in the mix. You don't need one, as hens lay eggs completely independently, but for some people it feels more holistic to have at least one cock in the group. Here's what you should consider:

**Roosters crow really, really loudly.** They do this every morning without fail. Your neighbors will hate you.

**Roosters are aggressive.** They will attack anything they feel threatens the flock. This is sometimes good and sometimes bad. My mother-in-law got attacked from behind.

**Roosters kind of beat up on the chickens.** They take *Fifty Shades of Grey* to a whole different level.

**Roosters make baby chicks.** They do this by fertilizing the eggs while they are in with the hens. Your chickens will produce lots of eggs without a rooster, but there just won't be any baby chicks without a daddy. Beware . . . the process of fertilizing the eggs is definitely not a gentle and tender moment.

# Ordering Chickens

Order your chickens from a local provider to make sure you get chickens that are suited to your region, and so that you have a local resource to contact for advice if you get into trouble. The best way to find a local chicken provider is to research who sells chicken feed in your area and ask them where people get their chickens. I got lucky—I have one of the best rare-poultry growers living 30 minutes away—but some chicken hobbyists drive hours for the hard-to-find breeds.

When buying chickens, you really have two options:

**Chicks.** Most breeders sell the birds as 3-day-old chicks. Bonding with your chicks is a big part of the process because it helps them grow to trust you. Plus, they're so damn cute you just want to cuddle them. The downside: Baby chicks (like all babies) are fragile, susceptible to an assortment of illnesses and basically need your help for everything. For the first few days, plan on spending 5 minutes out of every waking hour checking on them. Once everyone has settled in, you can move to checking on them every few hours instead.

**Ready-to-lay chickens.** Your other option is to order ready-to-lay chickens that are older and more stable in terms of health. As adult birds, they are pretty low maintenance. Your biggest challenge will be to get them to trust you, because you are a stranger and they have already spent the last 10 months in a routine they know.

# CARING FOR CHICKS & CHICKENS

I f you are getting chicks for the first time and are planning to raise them without the help of a mother hen, then you need to be prepared. It is not as easy as bringing them home and freeing them into the coop to fend for themselves. You are now the baby mama and with that awesome title comes some significant responsibilities. You are in charge until they can go in the coop, which can take up to 10 weeks, and they don't get to be free-range for at least 5 months, so be prepared to provide housing, heat lamps, food and water dishes and bedding for your new feathered babies.

## Home for Your Chicks

Start with a temporary home for your chicks. This doesn't have to be fancy, but it does need to have tall sides, a waterproof bottom and allow for airflow, while still protecting the chicks and keeping them warm. I like to use a big plastic storage bin. It's perfect for cleaning out because nothing sticks to the bottom or the sides. (Yes . . . there will be poop on the walls . . . and no . . . I have no idea how they can poop on a vertical surface.)

I always put a mesh covering over my chick house and securely pin it into place using clothespins or even large paper clips. Choose a mesh that is strong enough to keep other animals and small children out of the bin but is also not flammable. (I'll explain more on this one soon.) Next, fill your container with just a few inches of cedar or wood chips. I've also had success using the paper scraps from my shredder. Just make sure that you use something absorbent and easy to remove once it's soiled. Also consider that your curious

**The absolute best way to raise chicks is to let their mama do it for you, because the chicks then just stay in the coop. If you have a hen willing to raise chicks, life is easy because she does all the work for you. Just be prepared that some hens do not make the best mothers. It is really important that you stay close in case the mother freaks out and you need to step in and foster the babies.**

chicks will probably try eating their bedding, so go with something safe. (Newspaper is printed using soy-based ink, so you're okay.) One big note of caution for you when it comes to bedding: Make sure to avoid bedding that is excessively dusty. Respiratory issues are common for small chicks and lots of dust in the brooder is really tough on their lungs.

## Heating

Chicks need to be kept warm, so you'll be investing in a heat lamp or a mat heater to keep them consistently warm. The perfect air temperature for chicks is 95°F. Me, I use a heat lamp because it is easier to adjust heat levels by raising and lowering the lamp into the brooder. I find that placing your heat lamp at one end of the brooder, away from the food and water dishes, is the best spot for it. Test your temperatures in the brooder BEFORE you introduce the chicks.

For the first 2 weeks it is crucial that the temperature be the same during the day as it is at night. I also keep an eye on my chicks and how they react to the heat lamp. If the chicks are all huddled under the center of the lamp, it means they are too cold and you'll need to lower the lamp a little. If the chicks are sleeping away from the heat, then you know that the brooder is too warm and you'll need to raise the lamp a little. This process of adjusting the heat lamp will continue as your chickens get bigger, right up to the point when they start to grow their adult feathers, which will help them regulate their own body temperatures. Ideally, you want to reduce the temperature in the brooder by 5°F every week until the brooder matches the ambient room temperature.

## Feeding

When it comes to food and water for your feather babies, invest in proper feeding and watering systems, which are available to buy online or at any farm store. These are designed to allow your chicks access to the food (see page 205) but will keep them safe at the same time. Chicks are messy little buggers. Be prepared to clean their dishes daily, sometimes twice a day. As the chicks get more mobile and active, I like to raise the dishes so that they are off the bedding but still reachable, ideally at the shoulder height of the chicks.

For the first 7 days, make sure that the brooder is well lit for 23 hours per day so that the chicks can find their food and water sources. After the first week, you can begin to reduce the light gradually, over a period of about 4 weeks, to get the chicks accustomed to natural day and night.

As the chicks begin to develop flight feathers on their wings (often in the first few weeks), they will be trying to get liftoff in the container. It's super important to keep the mesh lid on at this point. I had one little flyer escape over a 24-inch wall.

This is also a great time to introduce some simple foods like plain iceberg lettuce. Make sure it's washed and free from any chemicals before you give them a few pieces to try out. Other great foods for your chicks to try include mashed bananas, cooked oatmeal and chopped hard-boiled eggs.

## Spreading Their Wings

Their temporary home will quickly become too small for your fledgling hens. I usually move the bin to the coop after about 8 weeks. Once in the coop, I remove the chicken toddlers to a cardboard box and turn the bin on its side so that they can return to a familiar space as they begin to explore the rest of their new home. This is also the time to remove the heat lamp—provided the nighttime temperatures stay above 65°F.

**Important note: Chicks need a lot of water. This is key for them processing their specially formulated chick feed, which is the ONLY food you can give them for the first few months.**

## Health

When raising chickens, there are a few common problems that you need to watch out for:

| Ailment | Symptoms | Cause | Treatment |
| --- | --- | --- | --- |
| **Pasty Bum (blocked vent)** | Poop glues the tail flap over top of the anus and blocks the entire process. | Usually happens when the birds are stressed, or sometimes because of something they ate. | Gently wash the vent with warm water and repeat every few hours until the bird poops normally. |
| **Respiratory Illnesses (coughing, wheezing, trouble breathing)** | This sounds like the chick has a cold. | Usually caused by a dusty brooder. | Remove the cedar shavings and replace with paper towels. Clean the brooder with plain white vinegar. |
| **Splayed Legs** | The legs of the chick stick out to the sides, making it hard for the baby bird to stand. | This happens for several reasons, including a hard birth, incorrect brood temperatures or even low nutrients in the food. | This is a tough one to fix. Several experts say to use a bandage to create a loop around the legs to move them closer together. Success is sadly low. |

## Routine

Happy birds are awesome birds! Chickens get bored easily, and a bored chicken is a destructive one. Those talons and beaks are built for shredding and ripping things apart. Make sure to keep your clutch entertained with lots of different activities. I find that doing something different every day is the perfect way to keep them happy. Here is my current chicken schedule:

**Monday** Let the chickens out in the vegetable garden for an hour to hunt bugs and grubs. Keep the hose handy, though, and spray any birds that go after the tender greens. They learn to leave them alone quickly.

**Tuesday** Chicken tetherball! Attach a head of lettuce or cabbage to a string at the top of the coop so that it swings. The chickens will stand in a circle, taking turns trying to get a leaf. Usually lasts for at least an hour.

**Wednesday** Dust-bath day. I like to give my girls a bag of sand to play in once a week. I dump it, or a bag of garden soil, in the middle of the coop and let them scratch, scrape and roll in it.

**Thursday** Put fresh herbs in the nesting boxes. Adding mint and thyme is great chicken aromatherapy! The fresh herbs also have a couple of other purposes. In the wild, chickens build nests in herb patches, so this feels very natural to them. Also, keeping fresh herbs in the boxes helps to cut down on insects like fleas, which avoid the strong smells.

**Be Aware Chicken poop is a source of salmonella. In fact, lots of new chicken owners get sick from cuddling their chickens because of the salmonella that is on their beaks and feet. When handling them, remember that you can love your chickens—you just can't lo-o-o-o-ve your chickens!**

**Friday** Let them play on the lawn. Chickens LOVE to chase bugs in the grass. Crickets and grasshoppers are favorites. A bonus is this helps keep down the number of fleas and ticks that want to latch onto your other pets. Just make sure to keep an eye on the girls if they start eating plants in the perennial bed. Once they get started, they can be very destructive to plants like hostas. My girls even started eating the hydrangea bushes.

**Saturday** Corn-on-the-cob day! Giving your birds fresh corn that is still on the cob is great entertainment for them. Some chickens aren't into it, but mine will spend an hour making sure they get every single kernel off. Also consider peeling back the husk from some farm corn and drying it out in the sun. This helps the corn keep longer for your chickens' enjoyment.

**Sunday** New bedding day! The girls love to check it out, dig in it, move it around the coop and build fresh nests.

# Chicken Coop

The chicken coop is where your flock will feel safest. This is effectively their home, and the better it is built, the safer they will be. Plan to invest in a good coop. Chickens at night are not the smartest birds. In fact, they are totally dopey, making them an easy target for everything that wants to eat them. The coop is where they will instinctively go to roost (sleep) at night, so they need to be safe there.

The best coops have perches that are at least 18 inches off the ground. (Chickens like to be high when they sleep.) There are lots of amazing building plans online if you want to tackle your own coop, or you can go the route I did and just have a good one delivered right to your door! Mine came complete with a safe heating system and a solar door that opens when the sun is out.

The coop should also include nesting boxes. These are 12-inch × 12-inch boxes that you line with either straw or shavings, and they are the spots where your laying hens will drop their eggs. I am a huge fan of having the nesting boxes close to the door of the coop or having boxes with a separate door so that you can easily collect the eggs without a crusty chicken pecking you (yep . . . it happens).

Fill your entire coop with bedding (not just the nesting boxes). The bedding keeps the poop from sticking to the floor. This makes it easier to clean, so whatever you choose, the bedding needs to be good at absorbing moisture plus nontoxic, as the chickens will spend the day trying to stuff the bedding into the water dish. Me, I use wood chips, but fresh straw works well too. Other great options include cedar shavings, mulch, even grass clippings. I have read some different opinions on whether or not fresh herbs help ward off lice and mites. I personally have had great success using them, and my chickens seem to love laying their eggs on fresh oregano. Try it in a few of your boxes to see if your hens are fans of fresh potpourri.

## Keeping It Clean

The smell of your chickens will be impressive. Chicken shit is super high in ammonia, and when it gets hot from the sun, it gets beyond funky. I believe that the stench is a contributing factor in the banning of chickens in most urban areas. Plan on cleaning out your coop weekly to keep your chickens (and your neighbors) happy! Me, I put the coop at the back end of my property. Even with cleaning the coop regularly, you just can't stay on top of that *parfum*! To clean a coop, you need to remove all the shavings and give it a wash to reduce the ammonia. I like to use white vinegar for this as it is a natural disinfectant and really seems to cut through the stink, as well as the shit that sticks to the walls and the floor.

# THE REAL COST OF CHICKENS

I made the decision to buy chickens in November of 2014, before the trend of backyard chickens really took off. I thought that having some happy free-ranging chickens would be idyllic but also practical, since I would have all those fresh eggs that the experts say are both healthier and tastier. As a naive *citdiot* (idiot from the city), I happily placed my order for my first 10 chickens for a grand total of $49.85 and then added another five rare ones for another $35. Here's what I didn't know . . .

The first 8 weeks are going to require some specialty items that you will only use for chicks. These include housing, heat lamps, food and water dishes and bedding for your babies. **Total spent: $320**

Food for free-range chickens is free . . . during the summer! You let them eat what they can find in the garden and the lawn. For the other 8 months, you are on the hook for the cracked corn, organic feeds, heads of lettuce, cobs of corn, bags of oatmeal, even the chopped grapes and bananas that Mom insists they love. **Total spent per year: $385**

Everything wants to eat your chickens. If you make your own coop, go for a solid option that is insulated to protect your birds both from being eaten and from turning into Popsicles in the winter. If the responsibility of creating a fortress sounds daunting, plan to invest in a good coop from a local (or online) supplier. Mine came complete with a solar door, nesting boxes and heated roosts for winter. **Total spent: $2,250**

The smell of your chickens is impressive, as I've said. I would use the word *rank*, but on a hot summer day *rank* doesn't even do the smell justice. Make sure you can give your chickens lots of space so that the poop isn't concentrated in a single area. I built a great chicken run to give them lots of room to do their business but also to protect them when I'm not around to watch for predators. **Total spent: $685**

The average chicken lays 180 eggs per year and lays for about 3 years. I have 10 of my 15 chickens left. That means I should get 3,780 eggs from my 3-year investment. **Total cost per egg: $1.16**—which doesn't factor in the organic feed for the lifespan of the chickens after they go into retirement. *Ouch!* Truth is, you are NOT raising chickens to save money on eggs. You are doing it for the experience.

## Protecting from Predators

Everything wants to eat your chickens. The cat from three doors away; the visiting dog that came at brunch with your guests; the vultures that circled overhead for several hours; the raccoons; and especially the weasels and their relatives! The horror stories I heard after getting the chickens were frightening. To date, I have lost a total of 5 out of 15 hens. This is to be expected, as it seems that most of these animals just want to kill the birds (not even really eat them).

Whenever you let the chickens out of the coop, you put them at risk of predators. If you want your girls to get plenty of fresh air but also want them to be safe, you might want to build a chicken run. Chicken runs are fenced enclosures that are ideal for daytime use. There are lots of options for chicken runs and the runs are simple to build for any DIYer. I built mine out of the evilest material possible (chicken wire). It is the shittiest material to work with when it comes to cuts and scrapes (I had them everywhere because it's sharp and kept rolling up on me), but chicken wire is also the best at keeping the bad guys out, because it is tough for anything (even big predators) to chew through. The best chicken runs have nice high walls, a roof to stop flying predators and wire buried at least 18 inches below the ground to stop the diggers.

## Outdoor Space

Chickens do best where they can have access to lots of green space, making big backyards ideal. They love grass, and the bugs in grass. They also love to eat your garden, dig in the mulch and roll in the dust and dirt.

Egg layers need at least 10 square feet of green space per bird to be happy. The key word here is *happy*! Mass poultry productions jam the birds into smaller spaces to increase the yield. Those birds are not happy birds, not even close.

It is possible to raise some smaller chicken breeds on condo rooftops; it's just important to keep them from overheating. (A hot chicken will pant and lie on the ground with its wings spread.) You can also raise chickens indoors, but keep in mind that chicken poop smells bad, really bad.

## Feeding

Even if you are planning to let your chickens roam free in the backyard, chicken feed is still important to have on hand so you can supplement their diets with some important nutrients that they aren't able to find in the grass. Chickens consume 6–10 ounces of food per day. In the beginning, purchase chick starter, which has everything that chicks need for the first

8 weeks of life. After that, these are the general terms for buying the right feed for the right age of the chicken:

**Starter Feed 1–8 weeks** (sometimes longer depending on the brand). These crumbs have lots of protein mixed into them to promote healthy growth. Try to avoid giving "treats" too early, as chicks need the nutrients in the starter feed before they fill up on things like lettuce and corn kernels.

**Grower Feed 8–18 weeks** (not needed if your starter feed is designed to feed them until laying age). This is kind of like teenager food for your chickens because its size is somewhere between adult and chick feed. It's considered the transition food to get your hens ready for laying.

**Layer Feed 18 weeks onward.** The main difference in this feed, other than the larger-sized crumbles, is that it has added calcium specific to egg production. This feed is only for adults, as it can cause kidney damage in younger hens.

## Life Cycle

Chickens can live to be teenagers, even though egg production for layers drops after 3–4 years. Having a plan in place for what to do with your birds for the next 8 years after they stop providing breakfast is a tough conversation for many hobbyists (me included). I figure that once you've named your chickens and created a bond of trust with them, then you're committed for the life of the bird … which includes the 8 years that they provide nothing but love. Make sure to consider this BEFORE you get backyard chickens.

## Chicken Sweaters

Putting your chickens in sweaters is awesome for everyone except the chickens! I had so many people send me beautiful handmade sweaters that I totally felt peer-pressured to dress up the girls. Of course, the upside was my social media exploded with chicken love. Before you dress them up, here is what you should know:

First, let's state the obvious: Chickens have feathers, kind of like a personal down-filled coat. You yourself don't wear a sweater overtop of a down coat, because you'd overheat. (See where I'm going with this?) If you have chickens that are good in cold climates, putting them in sweaters will screw up their internal insulating system. However, chickens often *molt* (shed their feathers) toward the end of fall. This is the only time that I'd consider helping them out with a little extra heat.

After I managed to get the birds into the sweaters, they all ran around trying to peck at one another and then at themselves. A healthy group of girls don't really appreciate the fashion. They really do attack the yarn! It was very stressful until I caved and got them all undressed. I didn't get any eggs that day. (Just sayin'.)

If the sweaters don't fit perfectly, your chickens are going to get tangled in them. I have one girl who is slimmer than the rest (more of a size 6 than an 8). She got her talons up under the hem and just stood there on top of the inside of the sweater, looking at me—and chickens are very good with the "look."

# ALL
# ABOUT
# THE EGGS

Raising laying chickens is really all about the eggs, and the real secret to the best eggs is happy chickens. If you are willing to spend time with your birds, getting to know them and their individual needs, then they will return the attention with perfect eggs that taste better than any store-bought option. Remember, chickens take at least 6 months to lay their first egg if you are raising them from chicks. If that seems like a long commitment, invest in ready-to-lay birds instead.

When people see my eggs for the first time, they always comment on how dark and rich-looking the yolk is compared with what they are used to. The secret to getting these deep-golden eggs is to let your chickens eat lots of dark-green leaves. I feed mine fresh sorrel and spinach from the garden, which also helps boost the nutrient levels in the eggs themselves.

## Egg Cleaning and Collecting

To wash or not to wash is a hot topic, with as many opinions as there are blog sites on raising backyard chickens. Here are some things you have to consider when deciding how you want to deal with your own eggs:

**Chickens can pass on bacteria and parasites.** Chickens are clean animals; however, there will always be creepy crawlies and bad things in the coop and around the areas that chickens have pooped in. Eggs laid in nesting boxes are exposed to these baddies.

**Eggs in nesting boxes will get dirty.** There is no way to prevent this. I am a huge advocate of building my roosts higher than the nesting box, because chickens will go to the highest part of the coop to sleep at night. By keeping your nesting boxes low, the hens are less likely to soil them as they sleep.

**Eggshells are porous.** Any dirt or poop that gets on them is pretty tough to get off, and if used in cooking, some of this shell may come in contact with the contents inside when you crack it. I even sometimes get shells into the food, which I then have to pick out.

**Storage.** When a hen lays an egg, she coats it in a natural covering that helps prevent bacteria from entering the egg. Called *bloom*, this substance also works to help the contents of the egg stay moist, acting as a natural preservative. Eggs with the bloom on the shell can be kept safely outside a refrigerator for several weeks. Store-bought eggs have the bloom removed and need to be kept refrigerated until you use them.

I don't wash my eggs until right before I use them. When washing your eggs, there are several expensive store-bought options that are available, or you can try my cheaper choices:

> **White vinegar.** This is a natural disinfectant. Using a little on a paper towel or cloth is a simple way to clean your eggs. DON'T do this until you are ready to eat the egg, as the vinegar can break down the shell, making it soft and spongy.
>
> **Plain soapy water.** Easy and simple, I use warm water and an eco/glycerin-based soap to clean my eggs. Avoid cold water, as some studies have shown that this opens the pores of the shell and creates a vacuum effect that encourages bacteria to enter the egg.
>
> **Sandpaper.** Great for wood . . . and eggs! A low-grit sandpaper is a great way of keeping your eggs dry, while removing all the stuck-on crap from the sides. Dry eggs stay fresh longer because more of the bloom is intact.

To keep your eggs as clean as possible, plan on collecting daily. You'll begin to see a routine as to when certain hens like to lay and which boxes they choose. Some hens don't like to lay an egg in a nesting box that already has an egg in it. I have one hen that will lay her eggs just outside the box if an egg is already in it.

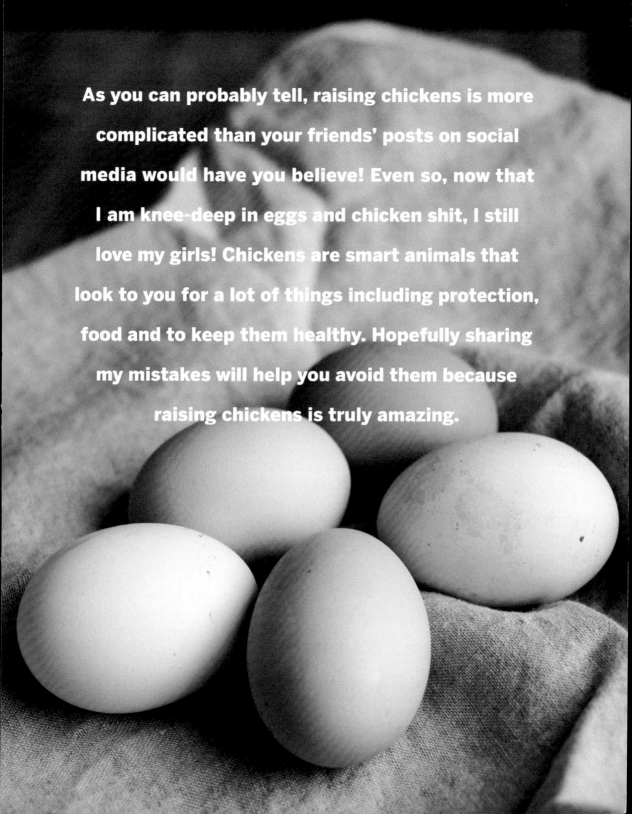

As you can probably tell, raising chickens is more complicated than your friends' posts on social media would have you believe! Even so, now that I am knee-deep in eggs and chicken shit, I still love my girls! Chickens are smart animals that look to you for a lot of things including protection, food and to keep them healthy. Hopefully sharing my mistakes will help you avoid them because raising chickens is truly amazing.

BEES

Keeping bees could be the single most important thing you do to make your space more sustainable. Bees worldwide are on the decline and need our help to survive—and we need bees just as much as they need us. This section will help you decide if beekeeping is right for you.

# CHOOSING
# BEES

All around the world we continue to hear about the plight of bees. SAVE THE BEES and COLONY COLLAPSE DISORDER (where entire colonies of healthy bees are dying for no apparent reason) are pretty important things to pay attention to, because up to 90 percent of the food that we eat is pollinated by bees. This is part of the reason that more people are getting into beekeeping . . . me included! It's also just really awesome and invigorating! The first time you put on a bee suit and open a hive is life changing. There is that moment when you realize that if this all goes wrong, you are going to get swarmed! But once you take a deep breath and realize that you got this, you begin to see that bees are phenomenal creatures, and that a happy hive is something very special.

Many local, state and provincial governments have set up rules and regulations for keeping bees. The first things to look at when contemplating beekeeping are the guidelines for your area. As part of a global bee protection movement, beekeepers are being asked to document how many hives they have and the state of those hives. Even though each site is unique, they are all good for sharing information from other local beekeepers about the state of their bees and what problems they are having.

## Queen Bee

Every hive needs a queen, whose primary role is to lay eggs that later become the workers for the hive. She also controls the mood of the hive, so an angry queen makes for a riled-up hive. Breeders import queens from all around the world, looking for the perfect balance of larvae production and honey collection.

Queens don't last forever. After a few years of nonstop babies, any good queen taps out.

The hive can create another queen naturally, or you can introduce one. Queens can live up to 5 years (compared with just a few weeks for your average bee)—probably because they are spoiled rotten by the rest of the hive.

The drones, that is, the useless boys who don't even have stingers, just hang around the hive, looking after the queen's fertility needs. They also move from hive to hive, hanging out with other queens and sharing DNA to ensure genetic diversity. Drones are sort of a "one and done situation." They die pretty quickly once they have done their job and mated.

The rest of the hive population are the workers. These females do it all . . . literally. Not only are the workers in charge of nectar collection and honey creation, they are also the air-conditioning, the security, the cleaning crew and the water brigade. Being a worker is an exhausting life, which is why workers usually only last about 6 weeks before they die. This is also why the queen needs to keep laying A LOT of eggs to keep everything going.

| Species | Appearance | Pros |
|---|---|---|
| Carolinian | Dark in color, with brown spots or bands on their abdomens. | Colonies stay small over the winter but grow incredibly fast when pollen is available (known to swarm). They handle cold winters better than most others. |
| Caucasian | Dark bodies that are sometimes almost black. | These are the gentlest of the honeybees. Not as common, because they have a lower honey production, but great for first-time beekeepers. |
| Hybrid Bee | A blend of different varieties. | Very prolific bees that have been created by crossing different lines to promote honey collection, gentleness and immunity. |
| Italian Bee | Light yellowish or brown bodies. | Known for large colonies, these bees collect the most honey but also need the most to get through winter. Considered quiet and gentle. The most popular in North America. |

**POPULAR TYPES OF BEES**

# CARING FOR BEES

Bees are amazing creatures. They will travel great lengths for the nectar and pollen that they use when creating the honey, which feeds the entire colony. Many beekeepers have several hives in a small area, knowing that there are enough food sources nearby to keep all the colonies going. Fields, parks, meadows, even community gardens all represent a food source for your bees, as they can harvest the nectar from flowers, trees and almost any type of plant. Some beekeepers are now having hives in urban settings. This is amazing, because they are helping pollinate all the plants in our cities.

## The Hive

When it comes to hives, they are all basically the same (no matter what version you are interested in): a series of boxes with vertical panels that the bees use to store honey and to lay eggs in. The biggest difference between most commercial hives is the way that the honey is extracted from the panels. Most traditional hives use a "crush and strain" method of scraping the wax coating off the cell and then straining the honey out. There are devices that help remove the honey faster, but they are pretty expensive. There are all kinds of accessories and add-ons that you can buy for a hive to make your life easier: things like "excluders," which keep the queen from getting up to the honey panels and laying eggs in them. I went with newer technology: a hive that has a specially designed system of removing the honey without having to take the panel out of the hive, so it causes less stress to the colony.

**New studies now link feeding bees artificially to their having a weakened immune system. Only feed your bees if there are no natural options available to them.**

## Temperature

Bees like a hive temp of 95°F. They can heat it up by buzzing. (*No joke!*) If outside temps drop, the bees will vibrate to create heat in the hive. If the hive gets too warm, they will congregate on the outside until it cools off. If it doesn't cool off, they leave the hive. I moved my colony into a more shaded area after the entire swarm moved into the apple orchard. Luckily, I was able to coax them back, and they have been happy ever since.

## Feeding

Bees collect nectar and pollen to feed the hive. They feed the pollen, which is 40 percent protein, to the young to help them grow. They hold the nectar in their stomachs until the water evaporates and it turns into honey, which they store for later. Bees need this honey in the panels to survive on, and this is extremely important to know when you take the honey. Your bees must be able to refill the hive to withstand times when there aren't a lot of sources of food for them. I didn't really think about this when I harvested a lot of honey in the fall, right before winter. My poor bees got into a lot of trouble without a large quantity of food available for them. Fortunately, bees can survive on winter food supplements like sugar water (2 parts sugar to 1 part water). The trick is to keep the sugar water thawed when it is cold outside.

## Cleaning

The term *busy bee* is no bullshit. Bees clean up after themselves, with worker bees designated to maintain the health of the hive by keeping it shipshape. The one time that you may have to step in is after a long winter. Often, there are a lot of dead bees that need to be cleaned out from the hive for the next round of larvae to have a healthy start. The dead bees can attract unwanted wasps and other predators that feed on the carcasses, so it's best to clean them up quickly.

## Health

As a beekeeper, you are responsible for keeping your bees healthy. There are hundreds of books and websites devoted to this subject, because if we lose our global bee population, we're screwed. When it comes to bee health, here are a few things you need to watch out for:

# BEE HEALTH

| Problem | Description | Symptoms | Treatment |
|---------|-------------|----------|-----------|
| **Mites** | The largest problem facing most bee populations. Mites are tiny insects that lay eggs on living bees, and when the eggs hatch, the larvae feed on the bee. | Scattered brood throughout the hive. Signs of neglected or dead brood. | Several varieties of mite traps and chemicals available online. Some experts use powdered sugar to "dust" the bees. |
| **Lack of Food** | Bees can starve during times of drought when there are no nectar- or pollen-producing plants available. | A quiet hive with dead bees in it. Adults dead with heads in the combs. | You can feed your bees with commercially made food or by mixing 2 parts sugar to 1 part water. |
| **Lack of Water** | Bees need water to control humidity in the hive, break down crystallized honey or food high in sugar. | Quiet hive with lethargic or tired-looking bees. | During the hottest months of summer, supply your bees with a shallow water source near the hive. |
| **Wasps: The Enemy of the Bee** | In 4 hours, 30 wasps can destroy a beehive. The wasps feed the bees to their larvae. | The first clue that wasps are invading is bee carcasses at the front door of the hive. | If you can find the wasp nest, destroy it. Invest in a wasp guard, a mesh that prevents larger wasps from getting into the hive. |

**Routine** Visiting your hive on a regular basis is great for the colony but also awesome for your own sense of well-being. It's hard to describe the feeling of standing with a colony of bees, understanding the operation and being a part of it. When I'm with my bees, it's a form of therapy. It's a feeling of being part of a bigger whole and it grounds you like nothing else.

I try to visit my hive every few weeks to check on the bees' health and happiness. In between those visits, I just walk by the hive to make sure that everyone is happily coming and going.

## Bee Protection and Tools

Online is the easiest and cheapest spot to shop for bee gear, especially if you find a deal on buying the full gear in one go. That said, making connections with a local store is always a good thing. I use one that is about an hour away. Other beekeepers are always there and the shop owner is a great source of info whenever I get into trouble.

**Bee suit.** Buy a GOOD bee suit. One that breathes will make your life so much better. The best time to work on a beehive is when it's less full—usually the middle of the day, when all the bees are out collecting nectar. It gets stinking hot working outside in the sun on a beehive... trust me. A good suit has airflow, so if there is any form of breeze, you won't sweat as much.

**Protective clothing.** If you buy a full-body bee suit, then you have everything covered. If you decide to just go with the jacket, then you have to protect your legs! Thick pants are very important. Skinny jeans or any clothes that are tight to your skin won't protect you from stings. I learned this the hard way. When the fabric of your pants is touching your skin, the bee security detail can push their stingers through the fabric and into your flesh.

**Duct tape or Velcro bicycle straps.** Tape your pant legs closed. I didn't do this the first time and got stung up my pants! The straps used to keep your pants from getting caught in the gears of your bike also work really well and are easier to get off when you're done.

**Good gloves.** Go for flexible ones that will protect your hands from being stung. At the same time, being able to handle small things that require dexterity makes the jobs faster. I like the heavy-duty cloth or leather options. I've even seen vegan leather options that work very well.

**A good smoker.** Smokers help control the bees' swarming nature. The smoke triggers a reaction in the colony to save the honey from a fire, so all the bees run into the hive to start eating it instead of going into attack mode and protecting it. The best smokers are the ones that are easy to light... and stay lit. The last thing you want is your smoker to go out just when the hive decides that you shouldn't be there.

**A hive tool.** Like a flat mini crowbar, the hive tool helps you open lids, remove panels and scrape the sticky stuff off the sides of everything! Bees really like to glue shit down and they are very good at it. The hive tool has been designed to really deal with almost anything you may run into while doing maintenance and honey collection.

# ALL
# ABOUT
# THE HONEY

One of the best benefits of beekeeping is sharing the liquid gold that the bees work so hard to make. I use honey every single day as a natural alternative to artificial sweeteners and processed sugars. I'm also a huge advocate of the health benefits of honey, including a boosted immune system.

Honey is a wonder food on many levels. It can go directly from the hive to a cool, dark space, and last indefinitely without going bad. I usually try to use up my honey within a few years because the flavor starts to get a little "flat" as it gets older. Some store-bought honey is pasteurized, but I'm not a fan of this process since there is very little hard evidence showing any benefits and lots of proof showing that pasteurization strips the honey of all the good things, including the beneficial bacteria and enzymes your body needs.

## Collecting Honey

The Langstroth beehive requires you to remove honey-filled frames and replace them with empty ones that the bees can refill. This is a pretty simple process, but it does cause stress for the hive because you are basically stealing the bees' food. These types of hives have been around for centuries and many traditional beekeepers swear by them. Once you've removed the frame, you use a melting tool to heat the wax coating off the top of each storage cell so that the honey can be drained out before the frame is put back into the hive.

Honey is ready to collect in a Langstroth hive when more than 80 percent of the cells in a panel are covered in wax. Wax-covered cells let you know that the honey has been cured by the bees and that the moisture they need has been removed from the collected nectar. In your first year, you will only get a small amount of honey, at the end of the summer, because the bees need all the honey reserves they can get to make it through the winter. As your hive becomes more established, you can harvest more often throughout the year as the honey becomes more readily available. Generally, though, don't harvest after September.

## An Alternative Method

As I already mentioned, I went with a new style of hive. Instead of removing the frames or the waxy seal, the honey is harvested right at the hive, with minimal stress to the bees. The process is simple. The bees fill premade honeycombs in the hive through their natural process of nectar collection. Once the honeycombs are full, you insert a lever into the frame and turn it. This opens the cells by changing their alignment. Then gravity takes over and the honey flows out. The first time I extracted the honey from my fancy panel, I wasn't ready for how much would actually be coming out. I set up my collection tubes, turned the "key" to start the flow and stood there with a small canning jar. A few drips came out at first, and then the honey gushed ... and gushed ... and gushed. I had honey everywhere as I ran to get pots and jars and anything that would hold the liquid gold. I got 30 pounds of honey from my first panel!

# Who Knew?!

## SAVE THE BEES

*Add herbs and grasses to the mix. Bees don't just use flowers for food. Go for woody herbs like rosemary and thyme in your planters; and ryes, fescues and other grasses in the garden.*

If you're not ready to commit to having your own hive, you can still help the bees by creating a bee-friendly garden for them to come and visit. Here are some ways to do it:

**No space is too small for some extra flowers.** Consider adding some to your window boxes and balcony planters, even if you are on a top floor of a condo building in the middle of downtown. Bees will travel up to 6 miles in search of food—they've even been found on the top of Mount Everest! Plant purple, white, yellow and blue flowers especially, as these colors are the most attractive to a hungry bee. Oranges and reds work too—in case you're already committed to a color scheme.

**Include more native plants in your gardens.** Local bees have developed a taste for local plants. Kind of makes sense. They were here before us, feeding on the indigenous plants.

**Stop using pesticides in your garden.** We don't know conclusively that the drop in bee population is directly linked to various sprays or GMO crops; however, the research is casting some pretty dark shadows in that direction.

## In the Meadow

Bees don't really love the lawn (unless it's full of dandelions!), so if you have a bigger space, consider planting a wildflower garden. I decided to do a little good for the world and planted a meadow full of a combination of wildflowers. Now I have a space that gives back to nature in the form of pollen for my bees and all the butterflies. I know it isn't for everyone, but I describe my little piece of nature as "perfectly imperfect." It's hard not to run through it singing "The hills are alive with the sound of music."

If you are considering planting a meadow/wildflower garden, you'll need to:

**Remove the grass.** Before you can start planting seeds, find a safe and ethical way to remove any existing lawn. (Spraying the entire area with an herbicide defeats the purpose of doing something healthy for nature.) I covered my lawn with a series of heavy tarps to naturally smother all the grass beneath. It takes about 4–6 months to really ensure that the hardiest of weeds living in the lawn won't come back. Once you're done, till or plow the area to expose the roots of the now-yellow lawn to the sun for a few days. This will help your meadow start out with as few weeds as possible.

**Choose the right seed mix.** I was surprised to find that several of the mixes available online carried invasive species like purple loosestrife. Research the plants that you will be putting into your yard. The best mixes have a combination of perennials, self-seeding annuals and some biennials, which take 2 years to flower and reseed. Also check the square footage that each package will cover, if you're looking to plant a big garden or meadow, and buy double if you are planning to sow the seeds by scattering them by hand.

**Contain your garden if necessary.** Wildflowers are naturally designed to spread. (*And they will!*) Make sure that you have a way to prevent the seeds from ending up in your neighbor's lawn. I was lucky with a large copse of spruce backing one side of my meadow and the driveway on the other. I still have to keep an eye out for plants that spread using the wind.

**You still need to weed.** For the first 3 years of a meadow garden, you will have to pull out the invasive weeds so that they don't take over the space and to make sure the good plants get established. This is part of the reason that researching what plants are in your seed mix is so important—at least you'll know what should be in the meadow!

Whether you're planning a wildflower meadow, a vegetable garden, or even a few containers on your balcony, your local bees (honey or otherwise) will thank you.

# YOU GOT THIS!

Alright, I know that was total information overload! It may take you a couple of tries to grow the veggie garden of your dreams, but the results are worth it—and there's no shame in a *#gardenfail* or two along the way. Even pros like me screw it up all the time. Remember, vegetables don't care if your garden is perfect. They're going to do their best to thrive, no matter what you throw at them.

There really is nothing more rewarding than growing your own food. As a society, we need to get better at buying less and doing more for ourselves and our families, especially when it comes to our food. After all, food doesn't just come from the grocery store! Our homes, yards and even balconies all provide opportunities to grow our own sustenance.

Whether you choose to start with a few simple pots on the windowsill, or really go for it and try your hand at raising chickens, having fresh food you've produced yourself will absolutely improve the quality of your life. And the best part is, anyone can do it!

My goal with this book is to empower you and to help you avoid many of the pitfalls first-time gardeners tend to run into. Hopefully, you're feeling a bit better equipped now! There is so much out there for you to explore and try—you just never know where your successes will come from. So why wait? Get out there and start growing!

## Thank You!

A massive thank you to Lindsay, Robert and the team at Appetite for working through this process of getting the knowledge out of my head and onto paper.

   To all of the photographers who added content to this book, especially Johnny, Denise and Kevin—your ability to capture the moment helped this book go way beyond my expectations.

# Index